SCHOLASTIC'S GUIDE TO CIVICS

HOW AMERICA WORKS

Understanding Your Government and How *You* Can Get Involved

🪶 **Your Constitution** ⚖ **Critical Supreme Court Cases**
🎓 **Electoral College** ⊗ **Impeachment** 👍 **Every Vote Counts**
🌐 **Immigration: Who Gets to Be an American?**
⚖️ **Fighting for Civil Rights** 💬 **2nd Amendment** 📣 **Media Literacy**
📝 **Could You Pass the U.S. Citizenship Test?**

📖 SCHOLASTIC

Hugh Roome, Publisher
Elliott Rebhun, Editor

Educational Advisers
Ron Adams, Broad Meadows Middle School (retired), Quincy, Mass.
Maureen B. Costello, Education Consultant, Montgomery, Ala.
Claudia Ducic, Dobbs Ferry Middle School, Dobbs Ferry, N.Y.
Betsy Gotbaum, Citizens Union, New York, N.Y.
Joseph Karb, Springville Middle School, Springville, N.Y.
Eliza Edel McClelland, Education Consultant, Brooklyn, N.Y.
Andrew Liss, Thomas Jefferson Middle School, Edison, N.J.
India Meissel, Lakeland High School, Suffolk, Va.
Tracy Middleton, Hidden Valley Middle School, Escondido, Calif.
Andrea Davis Pinkney, Scholastic, Inc., New York, N.Y.
Katherine Schulten, The New York Times Learning Network, New York, N.Y.
Rhonda Watton, Templeton Middle School, Sussex, Wis.
Christian Wrabley, Greater Johnstown High School, Johnstown, Pa.

Content Consultant
James Marten, PhD, Professor and Chair, History Department, Marquette University, Milwaukee, Wis.

Cover design: Tannaz Fassihi
Interior design: Judith Christ, Three Dogs Design (www.threedogsdesignllc.com)
Page production and additional design: Kathleen Petelinsek, The Design Lab
Project management and additional editing: Josh Gregory, Editorial Directions, Inc.
Photo research: Erin Paxinos
Index: Tim Griffin
Proofreader: Melissa McDaniel
Fact checkers: Tonya Ryals, Joan Nassivera
Marketing: Danielle Mirsky, Ashley Doliber

A special thanks to Scholastic Classroom Magazines, especially the editors at *Junior Scholastic* and *The New York Times Upfront*. Many of their articles have been adapted for *How America Works*.

HOW AMERICA WORKS

Edited by Elliott Rebhun

TABLE OF CONTENTS

WE THE PEOPLE
ARE GREATER THAN FEAR

To Our Readers

To be a citizen without a basic understanding of the Constitution is to be a bystander rather than a beneficiary of American democracy. To give but one example, a majority of Americans can't name the three branches of government, let alone understand their interrelationship. This can leave people—whatever their political beliefs—railing against politics and politicians and the historic inequities of a "rigged system," without any sense that they can get involved and have a real impact.

Decades of declining attention to civics education have taken a toll on our collective understanding of America's government. How do we reverse that trend and encourage more people, especially young people, to participate in government and civic society and help effect change?

The editors at Scholastic have deployed an array of tools to rebuild student engagement in civics. *How America Works* is the culmination of these efforts.

This book and companion website are built upon best practices honed by Scholastic over a century of working with teachers and students. In order to connect with today's students, civics education must be engaging, active, and relevant to their lives. Simply telling students that there are three branches of government does not promote learning, let alone a desire to get involved.

Our editors know from experience that people build interest and understanding in myriad ways. For example, we've included lots of political cartoons which are there for enjoyment, but are accompanied by discussion points that add context. Each unit of *How America Works* also has a structured debate that invites readers to step out of their existing mindsets and examine a national issue from someone else's perspective.

Indeed, the book's most important role is to promote informed discussion, because our democracy can only work with open, thoughtful debate about the challenges that face America. Listening to and working to persuade others is, in fact, the very essence of civic engagement.

This is a not a textbook. *How America Works* is designed to engage everyone from avid readers to people who are challenged by intimidating blocks of text. That's why our editors produced graphic features such as "Your 5-Minute Guide to the Bill of Rights" and curated "The Art of Protest," with 11 pieces of thought-provoking art, each of which portrays a current or historical issue to inspire discussion.

How America Works brings many of the most poignant photographs of American history together in one place. Each image is designed to grab students' attention and convey knowledge about our history and government to even the most reluctant readers. To this end, the photo captions and annotations tell the story of America in the most readily accessible short-form prose.

Most importantly, this book takes full advantage of the "secret sauce" for which Scholastic is best known: the power of stories. *How America Works* tells dozens of stories that offer examples of Americans working, and often suffering, to make a better nation. It is our hope that these stories inspire readers to think about how their own efforts can better our nation.

I wish to thank all the editors, designers, and photo researchers at Scholastic who are forging a better path toward engaging Americans in learning about their government. In particular, it is important to recognize the brilliant editor of *How America Works*, Elliott Rebhun, who brings to this project decades of experience promoting civic engagement and telling the stories of the people who have shaped, and are shaping, our nation. Finally, *How America Works* would not exist without the concept, scope, and editorial resources provided by Scholastic's leader, Dick Robinson, who saw this project as a vital part of Scholastic's legacy as the company celebrates 100 years of promoting the principles of democracy.

Hugh Roome PhD
Publisher

UNIT · 1

The Declaration of Independence

What America celebrates on July 4th

FIND MORE ONLINE: www.scholastic.com/howamericaworks

"ALL MEN ARE CREATED EQUAL": Thomas Jefferson is considered the author of the Declaration of Independence.

"Free and Independent States"

The Declaration of Independence explained to Americans—and the world—why the 13 colonies were breaking away from Britain.

Although the first shots had been fired a year earlier, many American colonists still considered themselves British subjects in 1776 and were not ready to separate from Great Britain. But the Revolutionary War (1775–83) had begun, and Americans were inching toward the idea of independence.

The Second Continental Congress began meeting in Philadelphia, Pennsylvania, in May 1775, just a month after the first shots of the war were fired at Lexington and Concord, in Massachusetts. Almost a year later, in June 1776, Richard Henry Lee of Virginia offered a resolution: "That these United Colonies are, and of right ought to be, free and independent States, that they are absolved from all allegiance to the British Crown, and that all political connection between them and the State of Great Britain is, and ought to be, totally dissolved."

The **delegates** from seven colonies supported the resolution. The delegates from the other six colonies were not ready yet.

At the same time, the Continental Congress decided that it should explain why America was breaking its ties with Britain. It appointed a committee of five men to write the Declaration of Independence: John Adams of Massachusetts, Benjamin Franklin of

Pennsylvania, Thomas Jefferson of Virginia, Robert Livingston of New York, and Roger Sherman of Connecticut.

Adams had no doubt who should write the first draft: Thomas Jefferson. And Jefferson thought Adams should write it because he had been a leader of the push for independence. Adams refused, and he later recalled giving Jefferson three reasons why he should write the Declaration:

"Reason, first, you are a Virginian, and a Virginian ought to appear at the head of this business." (Virginia was the oldest, largest, and wealthiest of the 13 colonies.) Then, "Reason second, I am obnoxious, suspected, and unpopular. You are very much otherwise." Finally, "Reason third, you can write ten times better than I."

Why the Declaration Ignored Slavery

Thomas Jefferson was 33 in 1776, one of the youngest members of the Continental Congress and one of the quietest. He spent two weeks writing drafts of the Declaration.

Before the Continental Congress considered the Declaration, they had to discuss Richard Henry Lee's resolution about independence. On July 2, 1776, after much debate, 12 of the 13 colonies voted for independence. (The delegates from New York had not yet been given instructions from the state assembly on how to vote, so they didn't vote. Two weeks later, New York voted in favor.)

Jefferson listed 27 ways King George and Parliament had trampled on American rights.

The colonies had decided that they were no longer part of Great Britain. Then, for three days, the delegates pored over Jefferson's draft of the Declaration. About 100 changes were made, and about one-quarter of Jefferson's words were eliminated.

The most hotly debated section concerned slavery. In his draft, Jefferson blamed the king for bringing slavery to America. "He has waged cruel war against human nature itself," Jefferson wrote, "violating its most sacred rights of life & liberty in the persons of a distant people who never offended him." Some found it strange that Jefferson had included this passage because he owned more than 200 slaves at Monticello, his Virginia home.

But delegates from the southern colonies would not sign a document criticizing slavery. Some delegates from northern colonies, which profited from the slave trade, also refused to denounce slavery, and some owned slaves in colonies where it was still legal.

Benjamin Franklin and many other delegates wanted to keep the antislavery language. But they thought it was more important to pass some version of the declaration, and they agreed to eliminate all mention of slavery.

From Colonies to States

Even with the changes the Continental Congress had made, the Declaration was Jefferson's. At the top, he had written "The **unanimous** Declaration of the thirteen united States of America." The colonies had become states. Here are the Declaration's key points:

- Jefferson began the Declaration by explaining why it had been written: "When in the Course of human events, it becomes necessary for one people to dissolve the political bands which have connected them with another . . . a decent respect to the opinions of mankind requires that they should declare the causes."

"We must all hang together, or . . . we shall all hang separately" —Benjamin Franklin

- In other words, breaking away from Great Britain was such a big step that the world deserved to understand why.

- Next are the most quoted lines of the Declaration: "We hold these truths to be self-evident, that all men are created equal, that they are endowed by their Creator with certain unalienable Rights, that among these are Life, Liberty and the pursuit of Happiness": the basic rights to which all people are entitled.

Jefferson argued that no government can take away these rights. In fact, he said the purpose of government is "to secure these rights," and when a government doesn't do so, the people have the right to get rid of that government. That was the reason for the Revolution.

He listed 27 ways in which King George and **Parliament** had trampled on the rights of Americans, including "imposing Taxes on us without our Consent," "depriving us . . . of Trial by Jury," and "waging War against us."

Of course, the reality was that in 18th-century America, these rights did not apply to everyone. The Continental Congress itself consisted of all white men—no women, black people, or Native Americans.

And all Americans didn't magically get these rights the day the Declaration was signed. That involved a long struggle that in some ways continues to this day.

Jefferson concluded with a statement about American independence. The colonies, he said, are now "Free and Independent States," and "all political connection between them

MARTIN LUTHER KING JR. quoted the Declaration in his 1963 "I Have a Dream" speech in Washington, D.C. He called it "a promissory note to which every American was to fall heir."

and the State of Great Britain, is and ought to be totally dissolved."

On July 4, 1776, the Continental Congress voted unanimously to adopt the final version of the Declaration of Independence. The only delegate to sign the Declaration that day was John Hancock, the president of the Continental Congress. The other delegates didn't sign until August 2, and some didn't ever sign.

To the British, the Declaration was an act of treason. According to Franklin, "We must all hang together, or assuredly we shall all hang separately." In other words, if Americans didn't stay united, the signers would be considered traitors and hanged for their crimes.

Six Years of War

The United States had declared its independence, but it took six more years to win the war.

In October 1781, the British surrendered their main forces in the South at Yorktown, Virginia, and most of the fighting stopped. The official end of the war came with the signing of the **Treaty** of Paris in September 1783.

The Declaration of Independence speaks to the highest hope of what the United States can be. Though it says that all men are created equal, signing the Declaration did not instantly create a land where everyone was free and equal. Nearly two and a half centuries later, there's still work to do. Thanks to the Declaration, Americans have a clear goal for their country, something to work toward: liberty and equality for all. ■

The American Revolution:
7 Things You Should Know (but Probably Don't)

Here are some little-known facts the history books often leave out.

The Revolutionary War is likely one of the first historical events you learned about in school. By now, you may have studied it enough—or listened to the *Hamilton* soundtrack so many times—to think you know all there is to know. But the story of the nation's founding isn't as straightforward as it is sometimes portrayed. Here are some little-known truths about the fight for America's independence.

1. The beef wasn't just about taxes.

Starting in 1764 with the Sugar Act, the British Parliament imposed a series of taxes on the 13 colonies to raise money to pay for the costs of their defense. The taxes angered the colonists. Though officially ruled by British monarch King George III and Parliament in London, each colony had its own local government and elected representatives. The colonists believed it was their governments, not Parliament, that should tax them. That's why their rallying cry became "No taxation without representation!"

In other words, the real conflict was about who had the power to pass laws affecting the colonies, according to Matthew Skic of the Museum of the American Revolution in Philadelphia. "The colonists were upset the decision [on taxes] was coming from Great Britain and not the American assemblies," he says.

2. Paul Revere wasn't the only night rider.

One spring night in 1777—two years after Paul Revere's famous midnight ride outside of Boston—a messenger pounded on the door of the house in Fredericksburg, New York, where 16-year-old Sybil Ludington lived with her parents and siblings. The man said that British troops were destroying the nearby town of Danbury.

Located 12 miles away in Connecticut, Danbury was a key supply base for the Continental army. Earlier that day, about 2,000 British soldiers had ransacked the town, torching houses and supplies, and forcing the residents to flee.

The messenger had ridden on horseback from Danbury to reach Sybil's father, Colonel Henry Ludington, who was the leader of the local militia of farmers and

SYBIL LUDINGTON, 16, rode into the night to gather the local militia to fight the British.

laborers. The colonel's forces were needed to fight off the British, but his men were spread over many miles. Someone would have to ride into the night and gather them. After his long journey, the messenger was too exhausted, and Sybil's father needed to stay at home to organize his men when they arrived.

Fearing that Fredericksburg could be the British army's next target, Sybil mounted her horse and made the ride. At houses scattered across the countryside, she banged on doors, waking families and calling the men to battle. By the time she returned home just before dawn, her father's men were assembling nearby. Militiamen from the area were joining Continental army units as they rushed to Connecticut to fight.

In the end, the British forces got away. But Ludington's ride would make her a symbol of the role everyday people played in winning independence. Her story was kept alive by her family, and in 1880 one of her descendants shared it with a historian. From there, the legend of Sybil Ludington's ride has grown.

"She was a tough woman who did what she had to do," said historian Vincent Dacquino, who has written books about her. "[She was] exactly what Americans are made of."

3. George Washington almost lost his job.

Who would dare second-guess George Washington, commander of the Continental army and future first U.S. president? Plenty of people, actually. In the fall of 1777, after a string of

THE COMMANDER of the Continental army, George Washington, almost got the boot.

defeats, some Congressmen questioned whether Washington was the right leader. They debated replacing him with General Horatio Gates, who had won a big victory in the Battle of Saratoga in upstate New York in 1777.

But people loyal to Washington, including France's Marquis de Lafayette, defended him. When Washington got wind of what was going on, he confronted his chief rivals—including General Gates—and they backed down.

Washington succeeded in part because his devotion to his troops inspired their loyalty. For instance, in March 1783, some officers grew frustrated and discussed mutiny. Washington spoke with them directly—which persuaded them to squash their plans.

4. African Americans fought for the nation's freedom—and their own.

Historians estimate that 500,000 African Americans were enslaved in the colonies at the time of the Revolution. Enslaved Americans faced a hard decision: Should they choose a side and take up arms, hoping to gain their own freedom?

In 1775, the British promised freedom to enslaved people who escaped and joined the British forces. Thousands of them, regardless of whether their owners supported the British, risked their lives to try.

The colonists were more reluctant to recruit and arm black people. Eventually, more than 5,000 African Americans (both free and enslaved) served in the Continental army. Black soldiers "played a role in almost every significant battle," says Kenneth Davis, author of the Don't Know Much About History series.

After the war, the British evacuated about 3,000 former slaves who had fought with them to freedom in Canada. But many others were returned to their owners.

"Most of the slaves who served in the Continental army didn't get their freedom," says Don Hagist of the *Journal of the American Revolution*.

5. A French teen became America's best friend.

In 1777, a 19-year-old French **aristocrat**, the Marquis de Lafayette, arrived in America, itching to join the colonists' fight. Lafayette had no combat experience. What he had was a grudge against England: His father had been killed fighting British troops in the Seven Years' War (1756–63).

Lafayette offered to join the Continental army as a volunteer. With nothing to lose—and hoping to take advantage of his connections in France—Congress made the teen a general. "He was basically an unpaid intern," writes Sarah Vowell in her book, *Lafayette in the Somewhat United States*.

The French rookie's enthusiasm endeared him to George Washington, and the two became close friends.

Between battles, Lafayette wrote letters to French officials, relentlessly pushing them to support the Patriots' cause. Thanks in part to his efforts, France formally backed the Americans in 1778. French money and troops proved critical to defeating the British.

Lafayette played a role in the fighting as well—his troops helped contain the British during the Yorktown, Virginia, campaign in 1781 that helped bring the war to a close.

Indeed, writes Vowell, the Frenchman "turned out to be the best friend America ever had."

FRENCH FAN: Lafayette helped convince France to back the Americans against the British.

A GLOBAL WAR: Revolutionary War battles took place not only in North America and Europe, but also in Africa and Asia.

6. The Americans won—but not necessarily on the battlefield.

"When you look at it battle by battle, the Americans lost far more than they won," says Don Hagist. After all, the inexperienced colonists were up against a professional army. Why, then, did Great Britain surrender?

The British "didn't have a good strategy for how to put down a popular rebellion," says Hagist.

Even though the Americans were outmatched repeatedly, they persisted, aided by France and other allies. The war dragged on and on, eventually stretching Britain's resources to the limit.

7. The fighting didn't actually end at Yorktown.

It's popular belief that the war ended when British general Charles Cornwallis surrendered on October 19, 1781, in Yorktown, Virginia. But that's only partly true. The British did admit defeat, but by that point Spain and the Netherlands had joined the war against them. It took nearly two years for all parties to hammer out peace treaties. In the meantime, "an awful lot of fighting continued to occur," says Hagist.

An early version of the peace deal (the Treaty of Paris) was signed in France in November 1782, but getting the news to troops fighting far away took months. As a result, the real last battle of the war happened on June 29, 1783, off the coast of India. There, French and British fleets were attacking each other when a British ship flying a white flag arrived to tell them the war had been over for months. ■

NEW YORKERS pull down a statue of King George III after the Declaration of Independence was issued in July 1776. New York City was occupied by the British for much of the Revolution.

1776: Should We Declare Independence from Great Britain?

t's the summer of 1776. Decade-long tensions with King George and Parliament over taxation and representation and other problems with British rule have boiled over into outright rebellion and war. The colonists now face a life-and-death decision: Declare their independence and form a new nation, or bow to British rule.

Turn the page to see how the two sides present their arguments in this debate. →

DEBATE

We are a strong union of colonies and have proven our ability to thrive on this continent. We have been taxed as British subjects, but we have no representation in Parliament in London. It is time to throw off the shackles of British control and go our own independent way.

Without that representation in Parliament, we have no say in our own governance. For example, in 1765, Parliament passed the Stamp Act, requiring us to buy a stamp to put on every piece of printed material we use. The Stamp Act taxed newspapers, legal documents, playing cards, and even calendars. Protests, boycotts, and riots erupted.

While the act was later repealed, more such laws continued to be issued from London, inciting other protests and violent altercations, such as the Boston Massacre in 1770 and the Boston Tea Party in 1773.

Only local governments, like those we have established in each of the colonies, can properly represent us

> **For years, we have tried diplomacy to address our issues, but the king and Parliament simply ignore us.**

and decide how to tax us.

We have tried diplomacy, but to no effect. When the First Continental Congress met, it sent a letter to King George, asking that the colonists be given the same rights as Englishmen. The king ignored the letter.

The Declaration of Independence, which was approved by the Continental Congress on July 4, 1776, explained all the reasons for taking this dangerous step. It also outlines a vision for government that would ensure "certain unalienable Rights," including "Life, Liberty, and the pursuit of Happiness." No government should have the power to trample on these rights.

We will continue to fight, as we have for over a year—since the battles of Lexington and Concord—to make our independence from Great Britain a reality. ■

DEBATE POINTS

★ We have petitioned the king and Parliament but to no avail.
★ Only local governments in the colonies can really represent us and fairly tax us.
★ We have the right to be an independent, self-governing nation. There is no logic to being ruled by London, across the Atlantic.

We should not bite the hand that feeds us.

While we disagree about how we are being governed, we should not go overboard and separate from the most powerful nation on earth. We are not traitors. Britain has supported us and allowed us to develop a new society as we colonize a continent on its behalf.

When we have been in danger, the Crown has sent its army to protect us. It helped us defeat our enemies in the French and Indian War, and it has gone deeply into debt to do so. To raise money to pay this debt, Parliament imposed taxes on us. While it's true that we are not represented in Parliament, we have forgotten that the taxes were meant to pay for our defense. (And Parliament did repeal the Stamp Act, which shows it is willing to listen to us.)

The British army is the finest in the world. Do we really want to continue to face them in combat? Do we have the training, the soldiers, or weapons to challenge their power?

> **The British army is the most powerful in the world. We don't stand a chance against it.**

If we continue to fight, we will surely be crushed, as many countries around the world have learned. Our greatest leaders will be treated as traitors, tried, and executed. This is lunacy.

We colonists should focus on working within the current relationship. We consider ourselves Englishmen, and we must continue to lobby the king and Parliament to respond to our frustrations about our lack of representation in Parliament, their tax policies, and their leadership. We produce rich resources, including cotton, flour, and tobacco, but we depend on the British and their trade network to sell these goods.

Let us find ways to resolve our issues and work with our current government, thereby ensuring that we can all prosper. ■

DEBATE POINTS

★ Britain has protected us and our lands, and as British subjects, we owe the Crown our loyalty.
★ We do not stand a chance against the British army, which is the best in the world.
★ Our trade and our economy will suffer if we separate from British rule.

If Paul Revere Tweeted His Ride . . .

n "The American Revolution: 7 Things You Should Know (but Probably Don't)," you read about Sybil Ludington's critically important ride. A lot more famous is the April 18, 1775, midnight ride of Paul Revere, a Boston silversmith. The mission of Revere and his companions, William Dawes and Samuel Prescott, was to warn the colonial militia of the approach of British troops before the battles of Lexington and Concord. Here the cartoonist imagines if Revere tweeted his ride instead of yelling, "The British are coming!"

In the second cartoon, the topic is taxes. "Taxation without representation" was a rallying cry during the Revolution. The cartoonist is commenting on another aspect of taxes that was as true in colonial times as it is today. ■

Analyze the Cartoons

1. Who are the people in the top cartoon? What's going on there?

2. How does the cartoon comment humorously about Paul Revere's ride—and tweeting?

3. In the bottom cartoon, what is the cartoonist saying about taxation *with* representation versus taxation *without* representation?

4. Why do Americans pay taxes? What are taxes used for?

"You know, the idea of taxation _with_ representation doesn't appeal to me very much, either."

The Constitution

Can a 230-year-old document still work as the foundation of our government?

FIND MORE ONLINE: www.scholastic.com/howamericaworks

YOU CAN SEE
the Constitution
at the National
Archives in
Washington, D.C.

How "We the People" Created the Constitution

The Revolution ended with freedom from Great Britain. Now the new nation needed a government that could transform 13 colonies into the United States.

American soldiers whooped with joy on the battlefield at Yorktown, Virginia. It was October 19, 1781. The main British army in the South had surrendered to George Washington, leader of America's Continental army. This victory brought the major fighting of the Revolutionary War (1775–83) to a close. The 13 colonies would soon be free from British rule.

The colonies—now states—had formed a national government even before their victory. The Articles of Confederation spelled out the powers of Congress, which could make laws but could not raise money through taxes. There was no executive—a leader who could make things happen. The new nation was really a confederation—a loose partnership—of states. The government was too weak to truly unite 13 states into a single nation.

Alexander Hamilton was one of the leaders of the push for a stronger national government. He thought the U.S. needed an executive who was separate from Congress and would have the power to enforce laws, settle disputes between states, and lead the nation.

As concerns about the Articles of Confederation grew, representatives of the states met in Philadelphia—in the same building, now known as Independence Hall, where many of the same men had signed the Declaration of Independence in 1776, 11 years earlier. The plan was to improve the Articles. But in the end, the 12 states represented (Rhode Island didn't send anyone) scrapped the Articles and created an entirely new government based on an entirely new document called the U.S. Constitution.

Delegates from the states began arriving in Philadelphia in May 1787. When it became clear that simply altering the Articles of Confederation wasn't the answer, the outline of a new government—with three branches—began to emerge:

- The legislative branch, called Congress, would make laws.
- The executive branch, headed by a president, would carry out the laws.
- The judicial branch would interpret the laws.

Dividing the power among three separate branches would mean no one branch could control the federal government, which would share power with the individual states.

Details, Details!

It took four months of hard bargaining to figure out the answers to some very controversial details about how the new government would work.

Congress would have two houses. Delegates from larger states wanted each state to elect lawmakers to both houses based on their populations. Delegates from the smaller states opposed this, since they would get a lot fewer seats.

Even trickier was how to handle slavery. The slave states of the South wanted each slave to be counted as one person so they would get more seats in Congress. Northern states, with much smaller enslaved populations or no slaves at all, opposed this.

These issues were finally settled with the Great Compromise:

- Congress would be bicameral, meaning it would have two houses. The number of representatives each state sent to the lower house, known as the House of Representatives, would be based on its population. Larger states, therefore, would have more representatives in the lower house than smaller states.
- In what became known as the three-fifths compromise, for every five slaves, only three would be counted for the purpose of representation in the House (though none of the enslaved people could actually vote). In other words, only three-fifths of the enslaved population would be counted.
- In the upper house, or Senate, each state would have two senators, no matter the size of the population.
- While the Constitution recognized the sovereignty of Native American tribes, the

vast majority of Native Americans were not considered citizens and not counted for purposes of representation in the House. (Congress granted Native Americans citizenship almost 140 years later, in 1924.)

- The leader of the executive branch would be called the president and would be chosen by a system called the Electoral College. Each state would name electors who would choose the president. The number of electors each state had was the same as the number of lawmakers it had in Congress. So Connecticut, for example, had five seats in the House and two seats in the Senate. Five plus two gave Connecticut seven electors.

- Congress could remove from office a president who committed "Treason, Bribery, or other high Crimes and Misdemeanors." The House could vote to impeach the president (file charges against him). The Senate would then hold a trial; if it found him guilty with a two-thirds vote, he would be removed from office.

- The delegates also set a president's term at four years, with no limit on how many terms he could serve. (The 22nd **Amendment** in 1951 created a two-term limit.)

- Slavery caused great debate beyond the three-fifths decision. The delegates agreed that Congress would have the right to ban the overseas slave trade starting in 1808.

The words *slave* and *slavery* do not appear in the Constitution.

They also agreed that enslaved people who escaped to other states would be returned to their owners. Yet the words *slave* and *slavery* do not appear in the final version of the Constitution.

Then It Was Up to the States . . .

The delegates approved the Constitution on September 15, 1787, and two days later, on September 17, 1787, which we celebrate as Constitution Day, they signed the document and sent it off to the states to be ratified, or approved.

Nine of the 13 states had to ratify the Constitution for it to take effect. Each state would hold its own convention to decide.

In December 1787, Delaware became the first state to ratify the Constitution, followed by New Jersey and Georgia. But delegates in some states strongly opposed the new government outlined in the Constitution. They were called Anti-Federalists. Those who supported the Constitution, such as Benjamin Franklin, George Washington, and Alexander Hamilton, were called Federalists.

The Anti-Federalists thought the new government took too much power from the states. Federalists James Madison, John Jay, and Hamilton tried to convince the states to support the Constitution with a series of **anonymous** newspaper articles called the Federalist Papers.

New Hampshire became the ninth state to ratify the Constitution on June 21, 1788. And so the Constitution was approved.

The choice for president was unanimous.* All 69 electors voted for George Washington, who was sworn in on April 30, 1789. He promised to "preserve, protect and defend the Constitution of the United States."

The new government met in New York City, which was then the nation's capital. The Bill of Rights (see Unit 3), consisting of 10 amendments to the Constitution, helped convince the last two states, North Carolina and Rhode Island, to ratify the Constitution. Thousands of amendments to the Constitution have been have been proposed since 1791; only 27 have been approved.

Why the Constitution Is a "Living Document"

Key amendments include the 13th, 14th and 15th, which were added at the end of the Civil War (1861–65). The 13th Amendment outlaws slavery; the 14th states that anyone born in the United States is a U.S. citizen (see p. 195); and the 15th Amendment gives all male citizens the vote, regardless of their race.

The 17th Amendment (1913) gave voters the right to directly elect U.S. senators; the Constitution originally gave that power to state **legislatures**. The 19th Amendment (1920) gave women the right to vote.

It's not easy amending the Constitution; indeed, the Founders ** didn't *want* it to be easy. But it can be done. Along with the Supreme Court's ongoing interpretations (see Unit 5) of the Constitution, amendments help make the Constitution a "living document."

And that may be why—whatever its original flaws—more than 230 years after 39 delegates in Philadelphia signed their names to it, the Constitution continues to serve as the foundation of our government, our democracy, and our way of life. ∎

* *Members of the Electoral College voted in December 1788 and January 1789 in the only presidential election that spanned two calendar years.*
**Though the term "Founders" is widely used today, it was once common to call them the "Founding Fathers."*

We the People

of the United States, in Order to form a more perfect Union, establish Justice, insure domestic Tranquility, provide for the common defence, promote the general Welfare, and secure the Blessings of Liberty to ourselves and our Posterity, do ordain and establish this Constitution for the United States of America.

AFTER WINNING independence from Britain, Americans decided they needed a stronger national government. The Constitution (1787) was the result.

Your 5-Minute Guide to the Constitution

The Constitution created our government.
More than 230 years later, here's how it affects you.

On September 17, 1787, our nation's Founders signed a document that continues to shape Americans' lives today. That day, delegates to the Constitutional Convention in Philadelphia signed the Constitution.

The Constitution is the supreme law of the land. It set up the federal (national) government, as well as the federal government's relationship with the states and the American people. Amendments—which were added later—spell out important changes, including guarantees of specific rights. Here's an overview of the Constitution and how it works.

CREATING OUR GOVERNMENT

1 **America won its independence** from Great Britain in the Revolution. The 13 original states then established a federal government with very limited power.

2 **Leaders called for a conference** to form a stronger government. In May 1787, delegates from most states met in Philadelphia for what became known as the Constitutional Convention.

3 **Four months later,** 39 of the 55 delegates signed a new Constitution, which took effect when 9 of the 13 states ratified it in 1788.

SEPARATION OF POWERS

The Constitution outlines a system of checks and balances to make sure that no one branch of the federal government has too much power.

Legislative

Congress, which has two chambers: the Senate and the House of Representatives

KEY JOB: Writes the nation's laws

CHECK: The Senate must confirm the president's nominees for the federal courts and cabinet positions.

Executive

The president, vice president, and cabinet

KEY JOB: Enforces the nation's laws

CHECK: The president can sign (approve) or veto (reject) laws passed by Congress. The president appoints federal judges, including Supreme Court justices.

Judicial

The federal court system: the U.S. Supreme Court and more than 100 federal courts

KEY JOB: Evaluates the nation's laws

CHECK: The courts can overturn laws and executive orders they find unconstitutional.

WHO SIGNED IT?

Fifty-five delegates attended the Constitutional Convention. Meet three of them.

George Washington The first to sign the Constitution, he became the nation's first president two years later, in 1789.

James Madison He played such a key role that he's called the Father of the Constitution. He was the fourth U.S. president (1809–17).

Alexander Hamilton He's famous now because of the hit Broadway musical about his life. In the 1780s, his essays, part of the Federalist Papers, won support for the Constitution. ■

A Comeback for the ERA?

The Equal Rights Amendment would guarantee equality for women if it becomes the 28th Amendment to the Constitution.

After decades on the shelf, the proposed Equal Rights Amendment (ERA) is back. In the 1970s and 1980s, women's rights **activists** tried to win passage of the amendment, which would guarantee equal treatment of men and women.

The push began at a time when discrimination against women was widespread. Women were kept out of many jobs and were often denied bank loans to buy a house or a car, to cite just two examples.

Congress approved the ERA in 1972. It later set a 10-year deadline for it to be ratified. Only 35 of the 38 states (three-fourths of 50) necessary for ratification had voted to approve it by 1982, so the amendment seemed to die.

In 2017 and 2018, Nevada and Illinois became the 36th and 37th states to ratify the ERA. Then in January 2020, Virginia signed on as the all-important 38th state. That set up what is likely to be a political and legal battle, in Congress and the courts, over whether the amendment can be resurrected.

What exactly is the ERA, and why has it been such a hot-button topic for 50 years?

WHAT THE ERA SAYS

The Equal Rights Amendment contains three short sections. The most important is Section 1, which says: **"Equality of rights under the law shall not be denied or abridged by the United States or by any state on account of sex."** (Section 2 gives Congress the power to enforce Section 1; Section 3 says that the ERA would officially take effect two years after the date of ratification.)

94
Percent of Americans who support an amendment that specifically guarantees equal rights for men and women

HOW TO RATIFY AN AMENDMENT

It isn't easy to change the U.S. Constitution. The process is intentionally difficult, and there have been only 27 amendments in over 230 years. Here's how it's typically done:

PROPOSAL First, two-thirds of both chambers of Congress (the House of Representatives and the Senate) agree to propose an amendment.

VOTE Next, state legislatures vote on the proposed amendment.

RATIFICATION When three-fourths of the states' legislatures (38 of 50 states) have voted to ratify the amendment, it becomes part of the Constitution—and the law of the land.

DO WE STILL NEED IT?

Most Americans back the Equal Rights Amendment, but some don't think it's necessary. Society has changed a great deal since Congress approved the ERA in 1972. Today, women hold powerful jobs in government, business, and the military, but there is still inequality.

Many **conservative** groups oppose the ERA. They say it would mean the end of laws and practices that benefit women, like being exempt from the draft.

A 1970S BUTTON for the ERA

WHERE THE ERA HAS BEEN RATIFIED

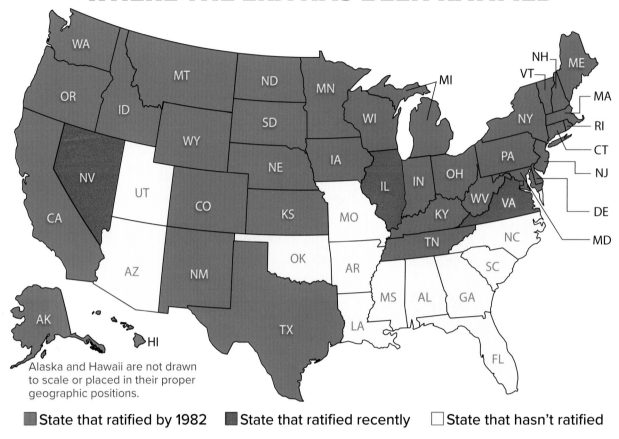

Alaska and Hawaii are not drawn to scale or placed in their proper geographic positions.

■ State that ratified by 1982 ■ State that ratified recently □ State that hasn't ratified

In 2017, Nevada became the 36th state to ratify the ERA. A year later, Illinois became the 37th, and in 2020, Virginia became the 38th.

What Happens Now That a 38th State Has Ratified the ERA?

Activists are lobbying Congress to ignore the 10-year deadline. ERA supporters point to the 27th Amendment, which Congress approved in 1789, and wasn't ratified until 1992! (It has to do with Congressional pay and had no time limit for ratification.) The recent ERA activity marks the first time a proposed amendment has won state approvals after a deadline. Getting the ERA into the Constitution is likely to be a major struggle, including court challenges and a fight in Congress.

80

Percent of Americans who mistakenly believe that the Constitution specifically guarantees equal rights for men and women

ALEXANDER HAMILTON wrote many of the Federalist Papers, which made powerful arguments for ratifying the Constitution.

1789: Should We Ratify the Constitution?

I t's 1787, and the United States has been independent for 11 years. The 13 states have been loosely governed by the Articles of Confederation. But there is no **provision** for an executive who could, among other things, lead the nation in a time of war. It's clear there's a real need for a stronger national government.

Delegates from the states, or most of them anyway, came back to Philadelphia to revise the Articles. Instead, they started over and replaced the Articles of Confederation with the Constitution. Nine states have to ratify the Constitution for it to take effect.

The Federalists are in favor of the stronger national government in the Constitution; Alexander Hamilton of New York is leading the fight for ratification. The Anti-Federalists, led by Patrick Henry of Virginia, think the new national government takes too much power from the states and are working to defeat the Constitution.

Turn the page to see how the two sides present their arguments in this debate. →

YES

We need a strong national government to thrive as a nation.

By dividing the powers of this new government among three branches, we ensure that no one branch, or person, will gain too much power. The system has built-in checks and balances so that the power of each branch is checked by the powers of the other two branches.

Under the Articles of Confederation, Congress did not have the ability to force the states to do anything against their will. General Washington called Congress "a half-starved, limping government, that appears to be always moving upon crutches and tottering at every step."

This Constitution will give the executive branch the ability to enforce Congressional acts. It will create a federal court system to settle disputes. It will give Congress two houses—in the House of Representatives the number of seats will be determined by population, while in the Senate every state will have the same power with two seats.

By outlining clear roles for every branch of government, the Constitution will prevent any one branch from gaining too much power.

> **We need a national government with enough power to create a true United States, not just a collection of states.**

A series of articles known as the Federalist Papers is making a strong case for the Constitution. They're written by Alexander Hamilton, James Madison, and John Jay (who are trying to stay anonymous so don't let on). Hamilton wrote that ratifying the Constitution was "the safest course for your liberty, your dignity, and your happiness." Indeed, the new, stronger federal government will make it easier for the country to defend itself from foreign attack and to grow its economy.

Many people are concerned that by giving the federal government new powers, we've taken away too much power from the states.

That's not the case at all. The Constitution makes the states key players. For example, every state, regardless of size, gets two votes in the Senate. And the Electoral College (see p. 110) is all about giving the states a key role in electing the president. ■

DEBATE POINTS

★ Each of the three branches of the federal government will check the power of the other two; that's why no single branch, or person, will have too much power.

★ Creating a strong federal government will allow the U.S. to defend itself—and grow its economy.

★ The Constitution outlines a clear set of powers as well as limits on those powers, protecting individuals and states from tyrannical rule.

 **It's been only a few years since we won a bloody war for our freedom from Britain.** Now some Americans want to create a central government with so much power that it undermines the authority of the states—and opens us to the possibility of recreating the tyranny that we fought so hard to escape.

Power should not be concentrated in the hands of a few people in our capital, New York City, and in the larger states; instead, as much power as possible should be in the hands of all the states and individual citizens.

Anti-Federalists are making strong arguments about how the Constitution prioritizes a powerful central government over the voice of the people. In the *Boston Gazette and Country Journal,* an anonymous writer tells us, "I had rather be a free citizen of the small republic of Massachusetts, than an oppressed subject of the great American empire."

With the Constitution as it is now, after much debate and struggle in Philadelphia, the president and the federal government simply have too much power—and it is power that will go unchecked.

What the Constitution needs is formal protections of individual rights and the powers of the states. In other words, it needs a Bill of Rights that guarantees, for example, freedom of speech, freedom of the press, and the right to a fair trial.

This Bill of Rights should also guarantee that any powers not specifically given to the federal government belong to the states.

We should not ratify the Constitution without such a Bill of Rights because we cannot risk the creation of a federal government that will have the power to oppress its own people. We fought the Revolution to escape just that. To accept an incomplete Constitution would be to jeopardize the freedoms we sacrificed so much to gain. ■

The Constitution gives too much power to the national government and not enough to the states.

DEBATE POINTS
- ★ We just fought a war against tyranny; let's not build a central government that could recreate that tyranny.
- ★ Power should not be concentrated in the hands of the federal government but with the states and individuals.
- ★ The Constitution gives too much power to the larger states.

Savvy Framers

Whatever issues we may have with the Constitution as it was written in 1787, there's no denying that the 55 delegates to the Constitutional Convention were a pretty sharp bunch. But of course they couldn't anticipate all the changes in technology and society that have taken place in 230-plus years, including cell phones, which are the subject of the top cartoon. They were, however, smart enough not to set the Constitution in stone, and they set up a mechanism to amend it when new issues arose. The Supreme Court also established in 1803 that it had the power to interpret the Constitution.

In the bottom cartoon, Alexander Hamilton shows he knows something about public relations as well as the Constitution. President Andrew Jackson (1829–37) may be making way on the $20 bill for Harriet Tubman. Hamilton, who's been on the $10 bill since 1928, is pretty confident no one will try to replace him. ■

Analyze the Cartoons

1. What constitutional issues do you think cell phones raise?

2. How have the Constitution and the Supreme Court (see Unit 5) addressed these issues?

3. Why isn't Hamilton worried about his position on the $10 bill?

4. What do you think of the proposal to replace Andrew Jackson with Harriet Tubman on the $20 bill?

"NO ONE'S POSITION IS SAFE, GENTLEMEN – NOT WITHOUT A HIT BROADWAY SHOW."

The Bill of Rights

What all Americans need to know about rights the Framers thought so critical

"A Bill of Rights? — Don't you *trust* me?"

FIND MORE ONLINE: www.scholastic.com/howamericaworks

Your 5-Minute Guide to The Bill of Rights

The first 10 amendments to the U.S. Constitution are known as the Bill of Rights. The amendments outline the basic rights and freedoms of Americans, such as freedom of speech and religion, the right to bear arms, and the right to a trial by an **impartial** jury. Read on for a quick overview of the Bill of Rights, how it was created, and how it works.

JAMES MADISON

How the Bill of Rights Came About

1. At the Constitutional Convention in Philadelphia in 1787, some states (including New York and Virginia) agreed to ratify the Constitution only if a list of individual rights were added. These rights were meant to protect against the kinds of abuses Americans had suffered under British rule.

2. James Madison, known as the Father of the Constitution, wrote suggested amendments, or changes.

3. Madison drafted nearly 20 amendments. Ten were eventually approved by the states, and the Bill of Rights was ratified on December 15, 1791, three years after the Constitution itself was ratified.

12
Number of original copies of the Bill of Rights in existence today

Which Rights Do We Value the Most?
Americans were asked in a recent poll which amendment they think is the most important.

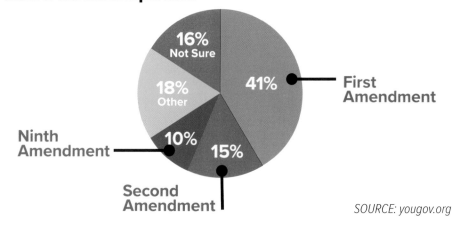

16% Not Sure
18% Other
41% First Amendment
Ninth Amendment 10%
15% Second Amendment

SOURCE: yougov.org

What Do the 10 Amendments Say?

1st Amendment: The First Amendment guarantees some of our most important rights, including freedom of speech, religion, and the press. It also protects Americans' rights to participate in protests and to petition (make a formal request of) the government.

2nd Amendment: The Second Amendment is about the right to bear arms, or own guns. What it means in the 21st century is a subject of intense debate.

3rd Amendment: The Third Amendment prohibits the government from forcing citizens to quarter (shelter) soldiers in their homes. Why? Before the Revolutionary War (1775–83), the British forced colonists to house their troops.

4th Amendment: This amendment protects people against unnecessary or unreasonable searches or **seizures**. Police must have a court-issued warrant or "probable cause" to search someone or their property. It also guarantees our right to privacy.

5th Amendment: The Fifth Amendment protects the rights of anyone accused of a crime. It assumes that everyone is innocent until proven guilty and is entitled to "due process of law." It also protects against self-**incrimination**: You can't be forced to provide **testimony** that might incriminate you; using this right is known as "taking the Fifth."

6th Amendment: Under the Sixth Amendment, Americans accused of a crime are guaranteed the right to a speedy, public trial and an impartial jury.

7th Amendment: The Seventh Amendment guarantees the right to a trial by a jury in civil legal cases in which damages are more than $20. (Civil cases involve noncriminal disputes between people.)

8th Amendment: This amendment prohibits cruel and unusual punishments. It also protects people from having to pay unreasonably high fines or bail—money given to a court in exchange for an accused person's release from jail before trial. (See p. 177.)

9th Amendment: The Ninth Amendment says that Americans have additional rights that are not listed in the Constitution.

10th Amendment: This amendment says that powers not given to the federal government by the Constitution belong to the states or to the people. ∎

First Amendment 101

More than 200 years ago, the Framers wrote the First Amendment to safeguard Americans' most important individual freedoms. What do these protections mean for you?

Disagree with a new law in your town? You can speak up about it. Worship differently than your friends do? You have the right to follow any faith you choose, or none at all. Want the latest scoop? Read as many news outlets as you like—or start your own. These are all rights outlined in the First Amendment.

THE FIRST AMENDMENT:

"Congress shall make no law respecting an establishment of religion, or prohibiting the free exercise thereof; or abridging the freedom of speech, or of the press; or the right of the people peaceably to assemble, and to petition the Government for a redress of grievances."

The First Amendment establishes Americans' freedom of speech, religion, and the press, as well as the right to assemble peacefully and petition the government for change. It's just 45 words—the text fits in a single tweet!

Yet the amendment gives Americans incredible power, according to Catherine Ross, a law professor at George Washington University in Washington, D.C.: "It gives us the right to criticize the powerful, to demand change, and to learn what is going on in our society so we can organize for political action and be informed voters."

1. FREEDOM OF SPEECH

Does the First Amendment allow me to say and wear whatever I want at school?

It's not that simple. School officials have the right to limit your clothing choices and speech if they think either might interfere with learning. But schools can't ban personal expression simply because it's controversial or unpopular. Case in point: In 1965 in Iowa, Mary Beth Tinker, 13, was suspended for wearing a black armband to school to protest the Vietnam War (1954–75). She sued the district, and the case made it to the Supreme Court. (See p. 90.)

The court ruled for Tinker, saying she had a right to peacefully express her views. In *Tinker v. Des Moines*, the justices declared that students do not "shed their constitutional rights to freedom of speech or expression at the schoolhouse gate."

Snapchat banned me! Isn't that a violation of free speech?

Nope. The First Amendment prevents the government and government institutions, like public schools, from punishing or **censoring** speech. But the rules don't apply to companies, private schools, or private people like your parents. ("You don't have First Amendment rights at home," notes Ross.)

Social media platforms may feel like public spaces. Still, it's perfectly legal for companies like Snapchat, Instagram, Twitter, and Facebook to block you as they see fit.

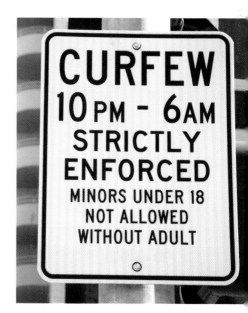

2. FREEDOM OF ASSEMBLY

My town has a curfew for teens. Doesn't that violate my right to peacefully assemble?

No. In fact, hundreds of U.S. cities have nightly teen curfews to help reduce crime and to protect teens. While the government can't decide who can gather based on a group's viewpoint, it can dictate the place, time, and manner in which people assemble.

TEEN CURFEWS ARE legal, most courts have ruled, to keep both teens and the community safe.

Curfews have been challenged on various grounds, including that they violate teens' right to gather. But most courts have upheld the constitutionality of teen curfews.

"The reasoning is that minors have lesser rights than adults, need to be safe, and . . . that the community also needs to be safe from disorderly young people," says Ross.

3. FREEDOM OF RELIGION

Is prayer allowed in public schools?

The Framers of the Constitution wanted to keep the government out of religion. They wrote what's known as "the establishment **clause**" of the First Amendment—"Congress shall make no law respecting an establishment of religion"—to prohibit the government from designating a national religion.

This means no religion can be funded by taxes or officially supported by the government. What does this mean as far as prayer in public schools? Generally, you can pray in school, as long as you're the one who initiates it and school officials aren't involved.

Do I have to say the Pledge of Allegiance? It includes the words "under God."

Schools are allowed to lead students in the pledge as a patriotic exercise, not as a prayer. But

YOU CAN DECIDE whether or not to say the Pledge of Allegiance.

whether you actually say the pledge is up to you: In 1943, the Supreme Court ruled in *West Virginia State Board of Education v. Barnette* that students have the right not to salute the flag or recite the pledge.

4. FREEDOM OF THE PRESS

We have to show the principal our school newspaper articles before we print them. Is that legal?

Yup. In 1988, the Supreme Court ruled in *Hazelwood School District v. Kuhlmeier* (see p. 86) that administrators have the right to preview and censor school-sponsored publications. School newspapers and yearbooks "are considered to be the school's speech, so the school does have a say in what's going to go in there," says Lata Nott of the Newseum Institute in Washington, D.C.

Administrators need to have real cause to yank articles, however. In the Kuhlmeier case, the principal pulled certain articles that he thought invaded some students' privacy.

Does freedom of the press allow the media to write whatever it wants?

Mostly. Journalists can cover anything they choose and from any viewpoint, whether impartial or intentionally **biased**.

However, there are two key limits. First, journalists are not allowed to knowingly publish false information about someone; that's know as libel.* Second, they can't print private information, such as medical or financial details, about someone unless the information is important for the public to know.

5. FREEDOM TO PETITION THE GOVERNMENT

Can I use social media to ask my classmates to lobby school officials?

In general, the right to complain to the authorities isn't up for debate. Just as we all have the right to complain to lawmakers, students have the right to lobby school officials. But you can't encourage actions that would disrupt learning.

How you make demands also matters, as Connecticut teen Avery Doninger found out. In 2007, she wrote a blog post urging fellow students to complain to school officials after they canceled a concert. But she insulted administrators in her post—and the school blocked her from serving on the student council. She sued, but the courts sided with the school, saying that Doninger's post had disrupted school for other students.

Learn from that, says Nott. "If your goal is to actually lobby the administration, leave out the insults," she says. Otherwise, "you're risking that your message will get lost." ■

---

* In general, libel *is a published false statement that damages a person's reputation;* slander *is a spoken false statement damaging to a person's reputation.*

BOSTON TEA PARTY, 1773: American colonists protested a British tax on tea—and "taxation without representation."

MARCH ON WASHINGTON, 1963: Dr. Martin Luther King Jr. gave his "I Have a Dream" speech before 250,000 people at the Lincoln Memorial.

WOMEN'S MARCH, 2017: Protests in Washington, D.C., and 600 other cities took place a day after President Trump's inauguration.

Protest Nation!

From the Boston Tea Party in 1773 to demonstrations about police conduct in 2020, America has always been shaped by protest movements.

t was a gray winter Saturday in Washington, D.C., but nobody was resting. Just one day after Donald Trump had been **inaugurated** as president in January 2017, the streets were jammed with people participating in the Women's March.

Near the U.S. Capitol building, they cheered speeches defending the rights of women and **minorities** who they believed the new president had disrespected during his campaign. Then, as if to make sure President Trump heard them, many of them marched to the gates of the White House.

The crowd in Washington, D.C., was estimated to have been around 500,000 people. Including the participants of more than 600 other marches held around the country that day, the Women's March was very likely the largest single-day demonstration ever held in the United States.

The gathering was part of "a long and proud history" of protest in the United States, says David Meyer of the University of California, Irvine. It all goes back, he says, to the first major American protest, the Boston Tea Party.

In December 1773, American colonists boarded three British ships and dumped 342 chests of tea into Boston Harbor. That act of defiance was part of a struggle over taxation and control by Great Britain. It also set the stage for a larger conflict: the fight for independence from Britain in the American Revolution.

"Protests seize . . . attention and force figures like presidents to respond to them," Meyer says. The tradition is protected in the First Amendment to the U.S. Constitution as "the right of the people peaceably to assemble, and to petition the Government." For the nation's Founders, who had led the country from resistance to independence, Meyer says, this was a sign of how much they valued dissent.

Indeed, says Meyer, "America was born from protest."

1965: A march for black voting rights from Selma, Alabama, to the state capital, Montgomery, was met with violence from the police.

Lots of Ways to Protest

Many of the most influential American protests have been marches, like the Women's March. Often, they have taken place in Washington.

A 1913 rally in the nation's capital for women's **suffrage**, for example, was a key step in securing passage of the 19th Amendment, which granted women the right to vote in 1920. The 1963 March on Washington, a defining moment of the civil rights movement, helped secure passage of the Civil Rights Act of 1964. That landmark legislation outlawed discrimination on the basis of color, race, sex, religion, or national origin.

Yet there are other effective forms of protest as well. During the long campaign for civil rights, great progress was made through acts of civil disobedience throughout the South. Boycotts of **segregated** buses and sit-ins at whites-only lunch counters (see p. 162) helped end many discriminatory laws and practices, often at great risk to the protesters.

As the barriers of segregation fell, the civil rights movement proved that protest could change society. It also created "a powerful narrative" of "protesters as patriotic [and] engaged in a just struggle," says Simon Hall of Leeds University in England.

From Vietnam to the (21st-Century) Tea Party

In the mid-1960s, U.S. involvement in the Vietnam War and a military draft ignited a wave of resistance among many Americans, particularly young people. They believed the nation was needlessly fighting in another country's civil war.

"Protests seize . . . attention and force figures like presidents to respond to them."

Inspired by civil rights campaigns, antiwar activists engaged in different forms of protest, including sit-ins at universities and the burning of draft cards (notices that a young man was eligible for military service). Marches were crucial. On a single day—October 15, 1969—about 2 million people rallied across the country to oppose the war. Historians say the protests were a major reason for the U.S. withdrawal from Vietnam that began in 1973.

Conservatives have also used protest as a tool to bring about change. In 2009, following President Barack Obama's inauguration, groups of concerned citizens began showing up at town hall meetings. Many objected to the proposed Affordable Care Act (also known as Obamacare), which they believed would boost taxes and health-care costs. The protests were also an expression of long-held grievances over gun rights, undocumented immigrants, and what some see as the government's expanding role in Americans' lives.

This new movement soon called itself the Tea Party, a tribute to the original American antigovernment protest. And Tea Partiers didn't just demonstrate. They also got involved in their communities and helped elect members of Congress. The Tea Party

WASHINGTON, D.C., 2017: Native Americans protested an oil pipeline that would run through the Standing Rock reservation in North Dakota and neighboring states.

brought an energy to the conservative movement that very likely contributed to Donald Trump's election in 2016.

The Future of Protest

Today, experts say, we may be in the most active time for protest since the 1960s. Meyer believes a new surge of resistance began in 2011 with the Occupy Wall Street movement in New York City. That started as an outcry against economic inequality in which thousands sat in for months near Wall Street, a symbol to many people of banking and wealth. The movement spread to other cities, energizing a new generation of young activists.

Protest gained more momentum with Black Lives Matter. This movement started in 2013 to address racial discrimination in the criminal justice system and protest the killing of African Americans by police. That issue also sparked nationwide protests after a man named George Floyd died while being detained by police officers in Minneapolis, Minnesota, in May 2020.

Donald Trump's election in 2016 also led to widespread demonstrations. Many people believed the president's policies threatened civil liberties—individual rights that are protected against government interference. Trump's supporters thought he would bring jobs and pride back to the United States. Both sides held demonstrations to show their point of view.

STUDENTS protest gun violence at the U.S. Capitol.

Protest Is What We Started With

Soon after his inauguration, scores of protests took place opposing the administration's attempts to ban travel from some Muslim-majority nations.

At the same time, conservatives held pro-Trump rallies and town hall meetings seeking to pressure lawmakers to repeal the Affordable Care Act and support the president's tough stand against immigration.

No one knows what will result from this moment in history. But one thing is certain, Meyer says: Americans are not about to stop reaching back to the spirit of the Boston Tea Party to try to shape the nation's future.

"Protest is what we started with," Meyer says. "It is an essential thing" for our democracy. ■

THE GADSDEN FLAG was one of the flags of the Continental Marines during the Revolution.

A RATTLESNAKE, coiled and ready to strike, became a symbol of the 13 colonies.

DONT TREAD ON ME

1

The Art of Protest

When it comes to swaying public opinion,
an image can be a very powerful tool

"**A**rt is for art's sake," goes an old expression. The artists represented on these pages might disagree with that idea. They have created works with a message—each image in its own way is an act of protest.

The pieces of art here tackle a number of issues, from the environment and war to guns and diversity.

These unique images were all created to plead, to argue, and maybe to provoke. Some of them may upset or even offend you. As acts of protest, their purpose is to make you react—and think about the world in a new way.

1. DON'T TREAD ON ME
The flag goes back to the American Revolution. The Tea Party, a conservative political movement that emerged in the early 2010s, embraced the flag as an expression of its resolve to protect individual rights. (In recent years, the Gadsden flag has also been used by some white nationalist groups which believe that the white race is superior to other races.) [Christopher Gadsden, U.S., 1775]

2. PARTY ANIMALS
This artist refers to the mascots of the major political parties—the Republican elephant and the Democratic donkey—without showing them. He seems to think that the choices our two-party system gives us are too limited. [Thomas Porostocky, U.S., 2004]

3. WAR IS NOT HEALTHY
In 1967, an increasing number of Americans objected to the Vietnam War, which many saw as a tragic mistake. One artist, worried that her oldest son would be drafted, created the most iconic poster of the antiwar movement. [Lorraine Schneider, U.S., 1967]

4. SCHOOL OR PRISON?
This poster—titled *How Can I Write My Own Future With My Hands Bound?*—tackles a complex subject: why so many black males end up in prison. The image may suggest that education is the key to freeing this young black man. [Mata Ruda, U.S., 2016]

5. GMO FOOD
Many people are worried about genetically modified crops—known as GMOs—in our food supply. This unpleasant image is a warning about the unknown consequences of messing with Mother Nature. [Jarek Bujny, Poland, 2004]

END
GUN
VIOLENCE

6. END GUN VIOLENCE
With a blood-red background and a stark message, this poster condemns the damage that firearms can cause. In the artist's view, gun violence casts a long shadow on many lives. [Jonathan Cumberland, U.S., 2013]

7. AGAINST GUN CONTROL
Gun-control supporters say gun-control laws keep guns out of the hands of bad guys. This poster uses a simple design and a surprising punch line to make a different point. [Zazzle.com, U.S.]

GUN CONTROL

BECAUSE CRIMINALS FOLLOW LAWS, RIGHT?

- WE THE PEOPLE -

ARE GREATER THAN FEAR

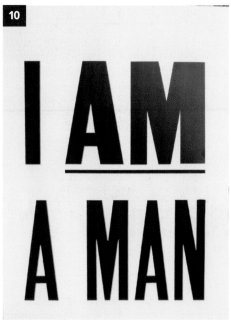

PROTECT THE SACRED

DEFEND
STANDING ROCK

8. OCCUPY WALL STREET

In 2011, many Americans protested the perceived greed in the financial system and the influence of the "1 percent"—the richest Americans—symbolized here by a Monopoly figure. Thousands staged a sit-in at a park near Wall Street in New York. [Lalo Alcaraz, U.S., 2011]

9. WE THE PEOPLE

This image of a Muslim woman in an American-flag hijab (head scarf) was created for the Women's March in 2017 as a symbol of American diversity, which many see as threatened by President Trump's policies. [Shepard Fairey, U.S., 2017]

10. I AM A MAN

Sometimes the most effective statements are the simplest. In 1968, black sanitation workers on strike in Memphis, Tennessee, carried this sign to assert that they were human beings with rights, not faceless trash haulers. [Unknown, U.S., 1968]

11. STANDING ROCK

In 2016, members of the Standing Rock Sioux tribe in North Dakota protested construction of an oil pipeline they saw as a violation of Indian land. This artwork presents a traditional Native American warrior in battle with a serpent that looks like an oil pipeline. [Jackie Fawn, U.S., 2016]

GUN RIGHTS ACTIVISTS display weapons in Texas, where it's legal to carry guns openly in many public places.

Do We Need Stricter Gun Laws?

n 2019, there were more mass shootings than days in the year, according to the Gun Violence Archive. Mass shootings have been on the rise over the past few years. Guns—many legally acquired—have killed people in schools, shopping centers, houses of worship, nightclubs, and public spaces. These shootings have stunned the nation, and each time, officials have vowed to reexamine gun laws, but little has changed.

Turn the page to see how the two sides present their arguments in this debate. →

In 2019, the U.S. had 417 mass shootings— the most in any year, according to CBS News. The U.S. ranks highest in gun violence of any developed country in the world. We also have one of the highest rates of civilian gun ownership. Yet when each new shooting occurs, lawmakers offer prayers for the victims and their families, with little if any effort to tighten access to guns. Instead, the burden to stay safe has been shifted to the most innocent players: Children as young as five now have to participate in lockdown drills in schools across the country.

Ninety percent of the population— including gun owners—support stricter background checks for people trying to buy guns. Most Democrats and Republicans agree that people suffering from mental illness, anyone listed on the no-fly list, or those with a record as a violent criminal should not have access to firearms.

Yet despite widespread support, there's been no real progress in recent years on restricting access for people who shouldn't own guns. The gun lobby, led by the National Rifle Association (NRA), is incredibly powerful, both in terms of the donations it offers politicians and in its ability to get supporters to the polls on Election Day. The result is that even popular measures such as background checks for potential gun buyers have made little progress.

The Framers guaranteed the right to bear arms in the Second Amendment for states that wanted to maintain militias for their defense. They didn't intend to give Americans a right to shoot their fellow citizens at will. They also could not have imagined the types of guns we have now.

According to the *New York Times*, "For men 15 to 29, [guns] are the third-leading cause of death, after accidents and suicides." If anything else were causing deaths at such a rate, the government would be undertaking significant measures to solve the problem. ∎

> **Ninety percent of Americans support stricter background checks for gun buyers.**

DEBATE POINTS

★ The U.S. has the most mass shootings of any developed nation.
★ The vast majority of Americans support background checks and common sense gun laws.
★ The Second Amendment was not intended to give Americans the right to own guns for illegal and immoral purposes.

 **The right to bear arms, as outlined in the Second Amendment, is essential to the independence and safety of the American people.**

In many rural communities, learning to use a firearm is not only recreational, it's part of a way of life. For generations, families have taught their children to use guns responsibly. For example, guns are used to protect livestock from predators and provide security in isolated areas.

Reducing access to firearms would primarily affect law-abiding people who respect the law even if they disagree with it.

The same can't be said about violent criminals who have already shown that they pay little if any attention to laws. Limiting access to guns will not deter those who commit horrible crimes; it will instead leave good citizens who could stop the crimes defenseless.

"Gun restrictions only keep good people from protecting themselves," says Erich Pratt, Senior Vice President of Gun Owners of America. "We don't need more gun control because no matter what laws get passed, criminals will still get firearms. Gun restrictions only keep honest people from using the best available tool to defend themselves. Guns save lives. But restrictions on firearms keep good people from protecting themselves."

Yes, most Americans support background checks, but how such measures would be implemented isn't as simple as it sounds. When the government starts issuing regulations, things can get complicated.

Individual firearm sellers should follow reasonable practices. But it is not the responsibility of the federal government to police gun sales. We do not want the government to determine how business is done between lawful companies and consumers.

Finally, if there is going to be more regulation of firearms, it should be at the state level, not the federal level. ∎

> ## No matter what laws get passed, criminals will get their guns.

DEBATE POINTS

★ The Second Amendment protects the "right to bear arms."
★ Gun laws limit law-abiding citizens from defending themselves, while criminals don't care about respecting laws.
★ Restricting access to firearms with government regulation is a slippery slope.

Two Views of the Second Amendment

High on the list of the most controversial topics in America today are gun rights and gun control. Horrific mass shootings in recent years have intensified the debate. Indeed, you may think that this topic is not something that should be presented in cartoon form. But cartoons can present serious arguments as effectively as text or even photos. Hopefully the two cartoons here serve that purpose.

The top cartoon speaks to the tricky question of what the Framers meant in the Second Amendment back in 1791, and how it relates to the world of the 21st century. It is something even the Supreme Court has struggled with, and indeed, avoided.

The bottom cartoon is making an argument popular with gun-rights **advocates** about who wins and who loses from gun-control laws. ■

Analyze the Cartoons

1. **Who do the people in the lifelike statues in the top cartoon represent?**

2. **What does the cartoonist seem to be saying about the meaning of the Second Amendment?**

3. **In the bottom cartoon, how do you think the cartoonist feels about stronger gun-control measures? Why?**

4. **Which cartoon more closely represents your views? Why?**

5. **Is it possible that both cartoonists are making legitimate points? Explain.**

How Washington Works

The three branches of government and how they interact

REPUBLICANS AND DEMOCRATS have long found plenty to argue about in Washington, but in recent years the "tug of war" has gotten a lot more intense.

Checks and Balances:
The Constitution in Action

Each branch of the federal government has great power. But our system of checks and balances means that no single branch, or individual, can ever gain too much power.

The Framers of the U.S. Constitution envisioned a nation in which no single person or group would have too much power. As a result, the Constitution established three branches of government: legislative, executive, and judicial. Each branch is separate and has its own responsibilities.

In addition, each branch checks and balances the power of the other two branches. This system is considered one of the most effective models of government in history.

Here's how the three branches operate—and how the three work together to govern our nation. ■

EVALUATES LAWS

JUDICIAL

THE JUDICIAL BRANCH is the federal court system. It is headed by the Supreme Court, the highest court in the nation. The court's nine members, called justices, review cases to interpret the law and determine whether laws enacted by Congress or the states violate the Constitution. They can overturn laws that do.

Supreme Court

A Supreme Court justice's **term of office lasts for life**. Justices serve until death, retirement, or their removal.

The Supreme Court **hears appeals** (requests for new rulings) of decisions made by lower federal courts. **Its decisions are final.**

Other Federal Courts

The **94 U.S. district courts** are where federal cases are tried.

The **13 courts of appeals** hear cases on appeal from district courts.

EXECUTIVE

ENFORCES LAWS

THE EXECUTIVE BRANCH, led by the president, handles the business of government, including the enforcement of federal laws. The president has the power to sign into law or veto (reject) bills passed by Congress. The president often draws on the advice of the vice president and cabinet members.

President

The president
- is elected to a **four-year term**.
- is **commander in chief** of the military.
- **nominates Supreme Court justices**, federal judges, and other officials.
- submits a proposed **federal budget** to Congress.

Vice President

The vice president:
- is elected to a **four-year term** on the same ticket as the president.
- **takes over the top spot** if the president dies or leaves office.
- **presides over the Senate**, casting the deciding vote in the event of a tie.

Cabinet

The members of this group:
- are appointed by the president to serve as advisers.
- **oversee federal departments**, such as Defense, Justice, and Education.

LEGISLATIVE

MAKES LAWS

THE LEGISLATIVE BRANCH is Congress, which is made up of two chambers: the Senate and the House of Representatives. Congress writes, debates, and passes **bills**. Bills that are passed by both chambers of Congress and then signed by the president become law.

Senate

100 Senators

- Senators are elected to **six-year terms**.
- **Each state has two** senators.
- The Senate **approves or rejects high-level nominations** that the president makes, such as Supreme Court justices.

House of Representatives

435 Representatives

- Representatives are elected to **two-year terms**.
- The number of representatives a state has is **based on that state's population**.
- Bills that deal with raising revenue (money) for the **federal budget** begin in the House.

A DAY IN THE LIFE OF . . .

A Member of

Ever wish that you were in charge and could write our country's rules? It's not as easy as you might think! Just ask a member of Congress. Read on to find out what a day as a U.S. lawmaker is like.

There are 540 rooms and 850 doorways in the main Capitol building!

8:00 A.M.

WELCOME TO WORK!

You're a representative from Pennsylvania. Like all 535 members of Congress, you work in Washington, D.C. Congress has two chambers, the Senate and the House of Representatives (which you belong to). Both meet in the U.S. Capitol. Together, they form the legislative branch of the government.

8:30 A.M.

PREPARE FOR DEBATE

Your key responsibility: to write, debate, and pass proposals for new laws, called bills. Earlier this year, you wrote a climate change bill inspired by a middle school class from your district. After months of meetings and revisions, your bill is ready to be voted on by the House. But first, representatives will be debating your bill, so you prepare your arguments.

9:00 A.M.

COFFEE WITH A BILL SUPPORTER

To get psyched for the debate, you meet with a fellow representative from Pennsylvania. There are 18 of you from Pennsylvania in the House. That's because states with large populations, like Pennsylvania, get more seats in the 435-member House. Each state gets two senators, for a total of 100. Overall, this ensures both large and small states are fairly represented.

10:00 A.M. → 10:45 A.M.

DEBATE

It's finally time for the House to hear and debate your bill. A majority of representatives agree with your proposal, and before you know it, it's time to vote.

HOUSE VOTE

For a bill to pass, a majority of members in both chambers of Congress must approve it. You vote "yea" (yes) for this one, obviously. A large majority of other House members do too. Your climate change bill passes in the House!

The House uses an electronic voting system, but the Senate takes an old-school approach: Each senator actually says "yea" or "nay."

Congress

12:00 P.M.
LUNCHTIME!

You've got to eat, but you also have work to do—so you wolf down a sandwich at the James Madison Memorial Building. It's home to the Library of Congress, the largest library in the world. You head there to do some research on NASA, the U.S. space agency, for your next meeting.

The Capitol campus is like a little city, with its own post office and banks. It even has a private subway system.

1:00 P.M.
COMMITTEE MEETING

The House has 20 different committees that consider bills and oversee programs and agencies, such as the FBI and NASA. You're on the Appropriations Committee, which helps determine what the government should spend money on. Today, you discuss how much to spend on sending astronauts back to the moon.

11:00 A.M.
ON TO THE SENATE!

Your bill's next step is a Senate vote and that could be months away. If a majority of senators approve the bill, it will go to the president to approve or veto (reject).

Only if a bill is passed by Congress and approved by the president does it become law.

(If the president vetoes a bill, Congress can override that veto with a two-thirds vote in both houses.)

5:00 P.M.
MEET WITH STUDENTS

You invited the students who inspired your climate change bill to travel to D.C. for the vote. You're thrilled to tell them the bill passed in the House! This is why you always wanted to work in Congress: to serve as the voice of Americans, teens included.

3:00 P.M.
RE-ELECTION PREP

You and your campaign manager brainstorm a new hashtag for your re-election campaign. Then you make phone calls to raise money for the campaign. House members are elected to two-year terms, so your next election is always right around the corner. (Senators serve six-year terms.) Holding frequent elections encourages members of Congress to listen to the people they represent.

A Changing Congress

New faces in the House and Senate after the 2018 midterm elections: 1. Rep. Antonio Delgado (D-New York) 2. Sen. Mitt Romney (R-Utah) 3. Rep. Alexandria Ocasio-Cortez (D-New York) 4. Rep. Sharice Davids (D-Kansas) 5. Sen. Marsha Blackburn (R-Tennessee) 6. Sen. Rick Scott (R-Florida) 7. Rep. Guy Reschenthaler (R-Pennsylvania) 8. Rep. Ilhan Omar (D-Minnesota)

Congress is starting to look more like America.

Congress is more diverse now than it's ever been. Of the 535 members combined in the House of Representatives and the Senate, 126 are women. That's the most ever, and almost a quarter of the total seats in Congress.

The number of African American and Asian American lawmakers has also increased. Other notable firsts include the election of the youngest woman* ever to serve in Congress, as well as two Native American women** and two Muslim women***. There are also more openly gay members (10 as of 2020) than ever before.

The newest legislators also come with a variety of experiences. Among the freshman senators and representatives in 2018 were teachers and former pro athletes. ■

Women and Men in Congress, 2020
Twenty-three percent of House members and 25 percent of senators are women. The Speaker of the House, who is second in line to the presidency (after the vice president), is Nancy Pelosi (D-California).

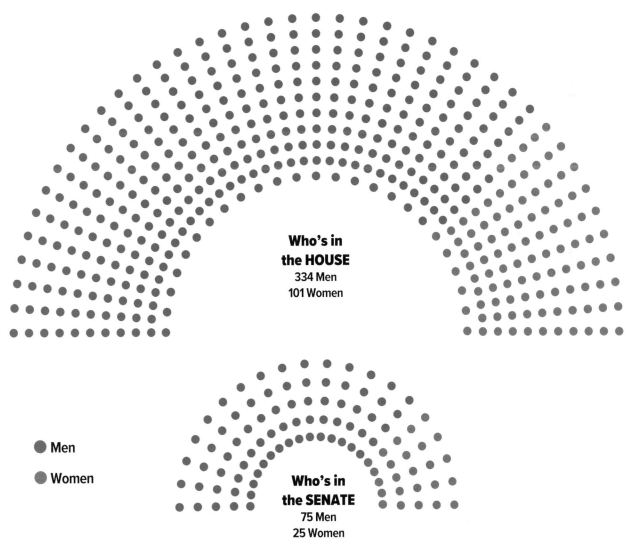

Who's in the HOUSE
334 Men
101 Women

● Men
● Women

Who's in the SENATE
75 Men
25 Women

Alexandria Ocasio-Cortez, D-New York, was born in 1989.
**Sharice Davids, D-Kansas; Deb Haaland, D-New Mexico*
***Ilhan Omar, D-Minnesota; Rashida Tlaib, D-Michigan*

MEET TAYLOR: Taylor Dalton is a cofounder of Students for Jahana Hayes.

MEET JAHANA: A former history teacher, Democrat Jahana Hayes is the first black woman to represent Connecticut in Congress.

"I Helped This Teacher Get Elected to Congress!"

By Taylor Dalton

Want to get involved in politics? Congressional and local campaigns are always looking for volunteers.

Imagine standing in a hotel ballroom full of cheering people and watching history unfold before your eyes. That's what I did on November 6, 2018.

It was election night. I'd spent six months volunteering for Jahana Hayes, a congressional candidate. As I listened to Jahana give a victory speech, I knew that I—and other students—had helped her win.

I never cared much about politics. But in 2016, I took a government class at school. At the time, the presidential election was under way and I enjoyed following the campaigns. It was a lot more entertaining than anything on TV!

But for the 2018 midterm elections, I wanted to do more than watch from home. So I Googled to see who was running for the U.S. House of Representatives in my district in Connecticut. That's how I found Jahana.

> **"I liked her positions on the issues that matter to me."**

I liked her positions on the issues that matter to me, like the environment. Plus, we live in the same town and she grew up in the city next to mine. I messaged Jahana on Facebook and asked if I could work on her campaign. She replied instantly, inviting me to help.

Jahana was a teacher, so she sees the potential students have. I got to do cool stuff. On primary night, I spoke with all of our poll standers. Those are the people who go to the polling places and get the final vote counts. As each number came in, I

Political Parties in Congress, 2020

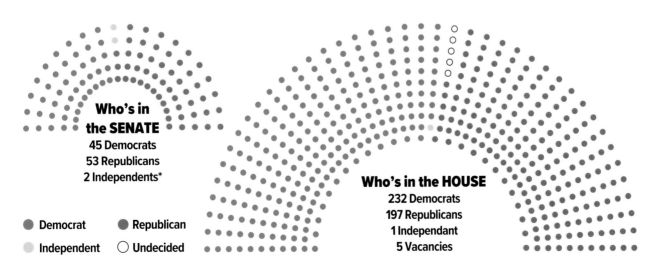

Who's in the SENATE
45 Democrats
53 Republicans
2 Independents*

● Democrat ● Republican
● Independent ○ Undecided

Who's in the HOUSE
232 Democrats
197 Republicans
1 Independant
5 Vacancies

* The two Independents in the Senate—Bernie Sanders of Vermont and Angus King of Maine—typically vote with the Democrats.

SOURCE: *pressgallery.house.gov and senate.gov*

entered it into a spreadsheet. It was so exciting! My heart was racing.

After Jahana won in November, I cried. I was really proud of what she had done and what all of us had done to help her. In her victory speech, she said, "There's an army of students behind me that made this happen," and she pointed to us in the crowd. We all just stood there screaming!

Jahana Hayes represents Connecticut's 5th Congressional District, which includes western and central Connecticut. She took office in January 2019 and is up for re-election in November 2020, like the rest of the House. Before entering politics, she was Connecticut Teacher of the Year and in 2016, National Teacher of the Year. ■

From the Classroom to the Campaign Trail

Hundreds of teachers ran for state and local office in 2018. Three of them explain why they got involved—and how their activism has inspired their students.

R. TRAVIS BRENDA	JESSICA CATES JANES	JOHN WALDRON
Republican, Kentucky	**Republican, Oklahoma**	**Democrat, Oklahoma**
"It's been exciting to see my students get excited about politics. They've taken an interest in government for the first time." Brenda serves in the state's general assembly.	"I always told my students to be the change they wanted to see. By running for office, I decided to be the change I wanted to see." Janes lost her race for the Oklahoma House.	"Being a teacher taught me to listen to people, to work together to solve problems, and to include everybody in making decisions." Waldron serves in the Oklahoma House.

Should Congress Have Term Limits?

The 22nd Amendment to the Constitution limits presidents to two elected four-year terms, but there are no restrictions on how long members of Congress can serve. Many have held their seats for decades. This has led to calls to amend the Constitution to impose congressional term limits.

Turn the page to see how the two sides present their arguments in this debate. ➔

DEBATE

YES **Politics should not be a long-term career.** Congress needs public servants who want to effect change and then make room for others with fresh ideas and the energy to turn them into reality.

Some members of Congress have held their seats for over 50 years. One reason this is possible is that incumbents—those who already hold a seat—have a huge advantage in elections. They have name recognition in their district or state and know how to connect with funders and supporters, so they have an easier time raising money.

Senators and House members should focus on the issues facing the nation, building alliances across party lines, and improving the lives of their constituents; they should not focus on raising money for their next campaign.

"Term limits would change priorities in Washington by putting an expiration date on each member's **tenure**," says Florida Governor Ron DeSantis, a former U.S. representative. "With a fixed number of terms, members would be focused on making their limited time in office matter."

> ## With a fixed number of terms, members would be focused on making their limited time in office matter.

Term limits would set a deadline on campaign promises by focusing politicians on completing the work they said they came to Washington to do. All too often, campaign promises are delayed, watered down, or even abandoned in the interests of getting re-elected.

Congress needs a steady supply of new ideas and perspectives. We have presidential term limits for similar reasons. Congress passed the 22nd Amendment in 1947—three years after Franklin D. Roosevelt was elected to his fourth term as president—and the states ratified it in 1951.

Term limits would also mean less opportunity for the corruption that often centers on helping politicians hold onto their seats. But first and foremost, term limits would create room for new players to rejuvenate Congress. ∎

DEBATE POINTS

★ Prevent career politicians by barring incumbents from holding their seats indefinitely.
★ Hold members of Congress accountable with a deadline for accomplishing campaign promises.
★ Provide more opportunities for new players and their ideas.

 **Running the government requires experience.** Politicians can improve with time, getting better at writing bills, developing relationships that build **bipartisan** support, and assembling a base of supporters so they can focus more on their legislative work and less on getting re-elected.

"Legislatures are where our nation's laws and budgets are written," says Thomas E. Mann of the Brookings Institution in Washington, D.C. "Doing that requires a level of experience and institutional knowledge that only comes from having served for a number of years."

Advocates of congressional term limits often point to presidential term limits. Term limits for a president make sense, but Congress is different. From a president's first day in the White House, there is enormous power in the presidency; having that power increase over time could represent a danger to democracy. In Congress, amassing that level of power simply isn't possible.

Turnover is already high in Congress. More than half of the seats turn over within a decade. And periodically, there is a game-changing election in which many incumbents end up losing their seats.

This is one way the system naturally corrects itself, and it's unnecessary to force these changes artificially. That would push out respected representatives and senators who have made lasting connections with their constituents.

If people in a district or state choose to keep electing someone, that's their choice. Term limits would set a precedent of Americans not being able to choose their own representatives, and that somehow, they don't know what's best for them.

It's not the place of the government to restrict the ability of Americans to choose whoever they like to represent them in Washington. ∎

> **Term limits would set a precedent of Americans not being able choose their own representatives.**

DEBATE POINTS
* ★ The government needs experienced politicians to effect change, and experience requires time.
* ★ Term limits would prevent successful politicians from continuing their work.
* ★ Lawmakers should reflect the will of their constituents and not be restricted by arbitrary time limits.

Why Congress Is No Laughing Matter

Editorial cartoons often focus on a particular person. (It's often the president, regardless of who's in the White House.) But cartoons can also take aim at the whole system, and sometimes they don't present a pretty picture.

That seems to be the case with these two cartoons. The traffic jam up top has nothing to do with a Beyoncé concert or a Washington Nationals game letting out—and there's no sign the gridlock is easing up.

In the cartoon below, it looks like the donkey and the elephant had a really nice dinner—but guess who gets to pick up the check? ∎

Analyze the Cartoons

1. What's the gridlock in the top cartoon about?

2. Can you tell who's responsible for the gridlock? And is anyone doing anything to get traffic moving again?

3. In the bottom cartoon, who just enjoyed what looks like a fancy dinner?

4. Who gets to pick up the tab? And what do the two diners seem to think about the bill payer?

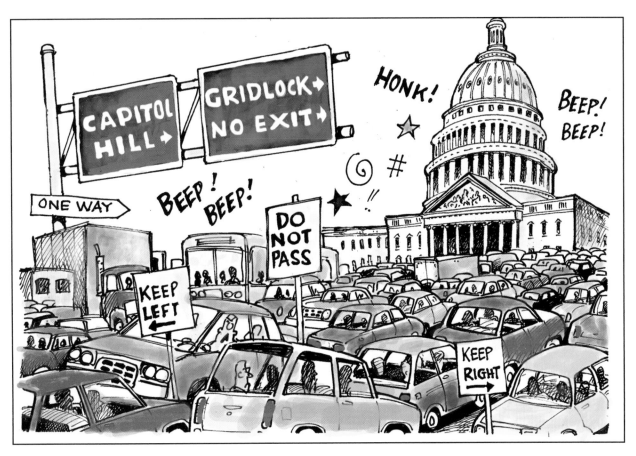

AN EXPLANATION OF HOW GOVERNMENT WORKS

Supreme Court Cases Every Student Should Know

The rulings of the nine justices of the highest court in the land affect the lives of every American.

NEIL GORSUCH,
1967; Colorado;
Donald Trump

SONIA SOTOMAYER,
1954; New York;
Barack Obama

ELENA KAGAN,
1960; New York;
Barack Obama

BRETT KAVANAUGH,
1965; Washington, D.C.
Donald Trump

STEPHEN BREYER,
1938; California;
Bill Clinton

CLARENCE THOMAS,
1948; Georgia;
George H. W. Bush

CHIEF JUSTICE
JOHN ROBERTS, JR.,
1955; New York;
George W. Bush

RUTH BADER GINSBURG,
1933; New York;
Bill Clinton

SAMUEL ALITO,
1950; New Jersey
George W. Bush

Justices are listed with the year they were born, where they were born,
and the president who appointed them to the court.

Your 5-Minute Guide to the Supreme Court

As members of the nation's highest court, the nine justices of the Supreme Court set precedents that all federal courts must follow. Their decisions become the law of the land and affect all Americans—including teens. The annual term of the Supreme Court of the United States (also known by the acronym SCOTUS) begins on the first Monday in October and runs through June or July of the following year.

Here's a quick overview of how the highest court in the land works.

The Supreme Court is asked to hear 80,000 cases each term. It accepts only about 80 which present issues of importance to the nation.

114

Number of justices who have sat on the bench since the Supreme Court was formed in 1789

OYEZ!

Pronounced oh-YAY, it means "hear ye!" It's shouted three times by an officer of the court at the beginning of each session.

HOW THE COURT DECIDES CASES

 ORAL ARGUMENTS First, lawyers on each side have 30 minutes to make public arguments. The justices frequently ask questions and interrupt each other.

 PRIVATE DELIBERATION Next, the justices meet in private to discuss the case and take a nonbinding vote.

 OPINION WRITING The most senior justice voting with the majority decides who will write the court's opinion (a statement of the decision); a justice in the minority may decide to write a dissenting (opposing) opinion.

 DECISION RELEASE The court doesn't announce ahead of time when a decision will be issued. It can be anywhere from six weeks to more than six months for a final opinion to be made public.

Life tenure

A term of office that lasts for life. In the case of the Supreme Court, the justices serve until death, retirement, or their removal. (See p. 99.)

How Americans View the Court

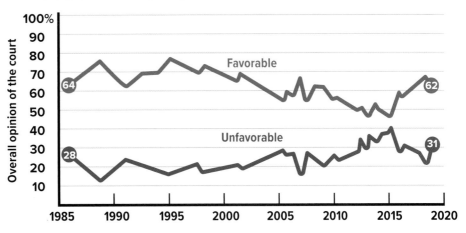

SOURCE: Pew Research Center, 2019

A DAY IN THE LIFE OF . . .
A Supreme Court Justice

What if you had to make a decision that would affect the lives of millions of Americans? The justices of the Supreme Court make those hard calls all the time. Read on to find out what a day as a justice might be like.

8:00 A.M.
WELCOME TO WORK!

You're a justice of the Supreme Court, the most powerful court in the country. Along with federal courts and judges, the Supreme Court forms the judicial branch of the federal government. The court's term runs from October through June or July. You work at the Supreme Court building in Washington, D.C.

The Supreme Court wasn't given its own building until 1935. At one point, the justices met in the basement of the U.S. Capitol.

10:00 A.M.
FIRST HEARING

All rise as you and the other justices enter the courtroom. When the Supreme Court hears a case, there is no jury—and no witnesses are called. Lawyers simply present oral arguments. Each side is allowed 30 minutes to argue its case.

8:30 A.M.
PREPARE FOR COURT

The Supreme Court's nine justices determine whether laws passed by Congress or the states violate the Constitution. If so, the court can overturn them. Before today's session, you look over the cases you'll be hearing. Most cases you hear are appeals, or requests for a new ruling on a lower court's decision.

1:00 P.M.

GET READY FOR VOTES

The public session is finished for today, but you need to prepare for a meeting later this week. You'll be leading the other justices in a discussion and voting on the cases you just heard. The most senior justice in the majority will decide who writes the statement explaining the court's decision in each case, known as the majority opinion. (A justice on the minority side often writes a dissenting, or opposing, opinion.) The majority opinion is the final ruling on the case.

Following British tradition, justices wear long black robes in court.

3:00 P.M.

REVIEW PETITIONS

Next, you evaluate petitions for new cases. The court is asked to hear thousands of cases each term but accepts only about 80. For a case to make the cut, at least four justices must agree to hear it. You're intrigued by an appeal to a digital privacy law. The case raises questions about how the 230-plus-year-old Constitution applies today.

5:30 P.M.

DINNER WITH THE JUSTICES

The justices often get together for meals. It's a chance to get to know one another better, although some of you have been working together for years. (Justices—who are nominated by the president and approved by the Senate—serve for life, or until they retire.)

12:00 P.M.

BREAK FOR LUNCH!

You pop by the Supreme Court cafeteria. The newest justice oversees the cafeteria committee.

Cameras aren't allowed in the room while the court is in session. A sketch artist records the action.

11:00 A.M.

SECOND HEARING

The second case you hear today challenges whether a climate change law recently passed by Congress is constitutional. By reviewing a law passed by Congress or an order made by the president, the Supreme Court both "checks" and "balances" the power of the other branches of government.

8:00 P.M.

BRING ON NETFLIX!

It's been a long day protecting the constitutional rights of the American people. Serving on one of the most respected courts in the world is hard work—and you're ready to zone out. Time to binge-watch *Judge Judy*!

Five Supreme Court Cases That Affect You

Many of the court's rulings have a direct impact on your life. Here are five examples.

Can Your Cell Phone Testify Against You?

In 2009, 19-year-old David Riley was pulled over by police in San Diego, California, because his car registration had expired. During the stop, police found two loaded guns. They also searched Riley's smartphone, where they found

photos and videos that linked him to a local gang. The police arrested him and seized his phone. Later, they found information on the phone that tied Riley to a shooting. He was convicted of attempted murder and sentenced to 15 years to life in prison.

THE RULING:
The police need your permission or a warrant to search your cell phone.

Riley's lawyers appealed his conviction. They claimed that because police hadn't obtained Riley's permission or a warrant before searching his phone, they had violated the Fourth Amendment, which prohibits "unreasonable searches and seizures."

The Supreme Court agreed. In a 9–0 ruling in 2014 (*Riley v. California*), the court overturned Riley's conviction.

Chief Justice John G. Roberts acknowledged that the ruling makes it harder for police to collect evidence. Cell phones "can provide valuable incriminating information about dangerous criminals," he wrote. But, he explained, "privacy comes at a cost."

Can Schools Require Drug Tests?

In 1998, 16-year-old Lindsay Earls was a model student. She was a member of the National Honor Society, the marching band, and the academic team. But at Tecumseh High School in Oklahoma, every student who participates in extracurricular activities has to agree to be tested for illegal drug use.

Lindsay didn't think that was fair. She reluctantly agreed to be tested so she could continue taking part in school activities. (She passed.) But Lindsay decided to sue the school district, claiming that its drug-testing policy violated the Fourth Amendment, which prohibits "unreasonable searches and seizures."

In a 5–4 ruling in 2002 (*Board of Education v. Earls*), the court sided with the school district. It said that "a student's privacy interest is limited in a public school environment, where the state is responsible for maintaining discipline, health, and safety." Drug tests, said the court, are "a reasonable means of furthering the school district's important interest in preventing and deterring drug use."

The ruling expanded on an earlier decision that allowed schools to test student athletes for drugs. Today, middle schools in a number of states conduct random drug tests.

THE RULING:
Drug tests are a legitimate way for schools to deter drug use.

THE RULING:
Schools can censor newspapers and other student speech if there are legitimate educational concerns.

Can Schools Censor Student Newspapers?

The First Amendment protects the right to freedom of the press. But if you write an article for your school newspaper about a controversial issue, it could get cut.

That's what happened in 1983 to Cathy Kuhlmeier, Leslie Smart, and Leanne Tippett—juniors at Hazelwood East High School in Missouri. When their principal refused to publish articles in the school newspaper about teen pregnancy and divorce, the girls sued. They claimed that their First Amendment right to freedom of speech had been violated.

In 1988, the case reached the Supreme Court, where the justices ruled 5–3 against the teens (*Hazelwood School District v. Kuhlmeier*). They said that a school newspaper isn't a public forum where anyone can voice an opinion, but a supervised learning experience that the school can control.

"Educators do not offend the First Amendment by exercising editorial control over the style and content of student speech," the court said, "so long as their actions are reasonably related to legitimate [educational] concerns."

Today, the ruling is often used to justify censorship of yearbooks, graduation speeches, and school plays.

Is Group Prayer Allowed in Public Schools?

For years, every football game at Santa Fe High School in Texas started with a student- led prayer over the public-address system. But that tradition ended in 1995 after two families sued the school district. They claimed that the prayer violated the First Amendment, which prohibits the establishment of a national religion—often referred to as the separation of church and state.

The Supreme Court agreed. In a 6–3 ruling in 2000 (*Santa Fe Independent School District v. Jane Doe*), the justices said that the prayer was a school-sponsored activity and that students were therefore being forced to participate in a religious ceremony.

"The Constitution demands that schools not force on students the difficult choice between whether to attend these games or to risk facing a personally offensive religious ritual," the court said.

However, the justices also said that "nothing in the Constitution . . . prohibits any public school student from voluntarily praying" on school grounds.

Today, the ruling is generally understood to mean that public-school students can pray together as long as their teachers, coaches, or other school officials aren't involved.

THE RULING:
Public school students can pray together as long as teachers and other school officials aren't involved.

Can Schools Search Your Belongings?

In 1980, a teacher at Piscataway High School in New Jersey caught a 14-year-old freshman smoking in the bathroom. The girl, whose initials are T.L.O., was sent to the principal's office. When school officials searched her bag, they found marijuana.

T.L.O. was arrested and convicted of selling drugs. Her lawyers appealed the conviction, claiming that her Fourth Amendment right to privacy had been violated. They argued that school officials should have obtained T.L.O.'s permission or a warrant before searching her belongings.

Five years later, in 1985, the case reached the Supreme Court. In a 6–3 ruling (*New Jersey v. T.L.O*), the justices sided with the school district. The court said that schools have the right to search students' possessions, including backpacks and lockers, if there is "reasonable suspicion" that a school rule or a law has been broken.

According to the court, schools must balance kids' "legitimate expectations of privacy" with the "equally legitimate need to maintain an environment in which learning can take place." ◼

THE RULING: Schools can search your belongings if there is "reasonable suspicion" that a school rule or law has been broken.

Three Cases That Changed America

Supreme Court rulings can have a powerful impact on everyday life.

1954: *Brown v. Board of Education*

The justices unanimously declared that public-school segregation—requiring that black and white children attend separate schools—was unconstitutional and "**inherently** unequal." Brown overturned *Plessy v. Ferguson*, an 1896 ruling that allowed segregation in schools and other public facilities if they were of equal quality, a **doctrine** known as "separate but equal."

2010: *Citizens United v. Federal Election Commission*

The court ruled 5–4 that spending for political campaigns is protected under the First Amendment. The ruling allows corporations and unions to spend unlimited amounts of money for—or against—political candidates. The money those companies and unions contribute has had a major impact on our elections.

2015: *Obergefell v. Hodges*

This case (and similar cases) resulted in the justices ruling that the Constitution guarantees a nationwide right to same-sex marriage. Under the 5–4 ruling, based on the 14th Amendment's "due process" and "equal protection" clauses, all 50 states must allow same-sex couples to wed.

STUDENT PROTEST: Mary Beth Tinker and her brother John with the armbands that made history.

1965: A 13-Year-Old Fights for Free Speech

Mary Beth Tinker's court battle helped guarantee your right to express yourself in school

As she got ready for school on a snowy winter morning, the quiet straight A student knew she was about to do something that could get her into trouble. But the 13-year-old believed she had no other choice. It was 1965, and U.S. troops were fighting in the Vietnam War (1954–75).

"All the time, we were seeing on the news: war, war, war," says Mary Beth Tinker, now approaching 70. "The bombings, the kids running from their huts screaming—it seemed like everything was on fire."

The more Mary Beth learned about the war in the Southeast Asian country, the more she wanted to protest it. So on December 16, 1965, she walked into Warren Harding Junior High in Des Moines, Iowa, wearing a black armband with a peace sign on it. Mary Beth meant the armband to be a symbol of mourning for both the Americans and the Vietnamese who had been killed in the war.

That didn't go over well with the principal. He said Mary Beth had disrupted other students by wearing the armband—and suspended her.

The Tinker family believed the suspension violated Mary Beth's First Amendment right to free speech and sued the school district. Eventually, the case made it to the U.S. Supreme Court.

In 1969, the court ruled 7-2 in favor of the Tinkers. The justices wrote that students and teachers don't "shed their constitutional rights to freedom of speech or expression at the schoolhouse gate."

Fifty years later, the case—*Tinker v. Des Moines*—remains one of the most important in U.S. history. It established that public school students can voice their opinions. Or as Tinker puts it today: "Young people can speak up about the things that affect their lives."

The Spirit of the '60s

Mary Beth grew up in the 1960s, a time when many Americans, especially young people, were pushing for big changes in society. "Kids today say they're 'woke,'" Mary Beth says. "Many young people through history have been woke."

In the 1960s, young people helped lead the civil rights movement. In 1963, for example, thousands of students marched in Birmingham, Alabama, to demand an end to racial segregation. The police released dogs to attack them and blasted them with water from fire hoses. Some of the young protesters were thrown in jail. But their courage helped lead to laws outlawing segregation.

"Young people can speak up about the things that affect their lives."

The Vietnam War moved students to action too. In 1965, the U.S. began sending combat troops to Vietnam. Most Americans supported the war at the time. But a small, vocal antiwar movement was forming—especially among young people.

As Mary Beth and her brother John, 15, heard about antiwar protests, they felt inspired. The siblings and three friends agreed to wear armbands to school to express opposition to the war.

"We saw young people standing up for the things they taught us in school and in church but weren't reality, like fairness, equality, justice, and peace," Mary Beth recalls. "That was a turning point for us."

But as Mary Beth, John, and their friends were planning their protest, school officials

Tinker has been "almost a Declaration of Independence for students."

learned about it. They quickly banned all armbands and said that anyone who broke the rule would be suspended.

The Tinker siblings and their friends decided to protest anyway. Expressing their views was worth a suspension, they reasoned. Still, they worried. On the day he wore the armband, 15-year-old Chris Eckhardt had a "dry throat and butterfly stomach," he later said.

As for Mary Beth, she thought she would just serve her suspension and then move on. "I had no idea," she says, "that our small action was going to turn into such a big thing."

The Tinkers Head to Court

The Tinkers didn't take the suspensions lightly. The family appealed the punishment to the school board. Hundreds of people showed up to the board's meeting. Some supported the teens. Others called their protest un-American. The board held firm: The Tinkers and their three friends were suspended. Case closed.

Still, the students and their parents refused to give up. Both the Tinker and the Eckhardt families opposed the war in Vietnam and stood behind their kids. With the help of lawyers from a group called the American Civil Liberties Union (ACLU), the families sued the school district. The case began to make its way through the courts.

At the same time, more men were being drafted into the military, and the antiwar movement was growing. In 1967, about 100,000 people demonstrated against the war in Washington, D.C.

WAR & THE HOME FRONT: A fireball erupts near U.S. troops in South Vietnam in 1966; young people protesting the war in Washington, D.C., in 1973.

However, many Americans still considered it wrong to oppose the war. As a result, the Tinkers became the focus of a lot of anger. The family received hate mail and death threats, and someone shattered their car window with a brick.

The First Amendment and Students

At the center of the *Tinker* case was the First Amendment, which guarantees, among other things, the right to free speech. The amendment's protections had been spelled out in the Constitution. But until *Tinker*, the courts hadn't considered how the First Amendment applied to students.

"Students were supposed to go to school and do what they were told," says Steve Wermiel, a law professor at American University in Washington, D.C. "It was unclear what rights they had."

Two years after the Tinkers filed suit in 1966, the Supreme Court agreed to hear their case. On February 24, 1969, the justices delivered their ruling: Students had every right to speak their minds as long as they didn't disrupt school activities.

"Our Constitution does not permit officials of the State to deny [students'] form of expression," the court's decision read.

What the Ruling Means Today

By then, Mary Beth was in 11th grade. After the long court battle, she was surprised, she told a reporter, "that important judges like those on the Supreme Court would rule in favor of kids."

The Tinker family celebrated that night with ice cream. "But I had sad feelings as well," says Mary Beth. After all, the Vietnam War, with all of its suffering and death, raged on.

A half-century later, how does the case affect you and other students? The nationwide student protests on March 14, 2018, offer one example. On that day, thousands of students walked out of their classes to demand an end to gun violence after a shooting at a high school in Parkland, Florida, killed 17 people. Schools wrestled with how to respond to the walkouts. Some officials helped students protest. Others threatened to suspend them.

Before the protests, the ACLU reminded students via social media that schools could

50+ YEARS LATER: Florida students protest gun violence after the shooting at Marjory Stoneman Douglas High School in Parkland in 2018.

punish them for not attending class. What schools couldn't do, however, was discipline teens who walked out "more harshly because of the political nature of, or the message behind" their actions.

The fact that schools can't punish students for their views comes from the *Tinker* case. The ruling gave students the right to "think critically for themselves and express themselves," says Wermiel. "It was almost a Declaration of Independence for students."

On the day of the 2018 walkouts, Tinker, now a retired nurse, joined student protesters near her McLean, Virginia, home. She told them to keep speaking up.

"When you find an issue that you care about, that affects your life, and you join up with a group of others to take action," she says, "then life becomes so meaningful." ■

So can I say anything I want in school?

You're probably wondering: Does the *Tinker* ruling mean I can say anything I want in school? Nope. The ruling ensures that students have free speech rights in public school. But school officials must balance students' First Amendment rights with the need to maintain order. So student expression is allowed as long as it doesn't cause a "substantial disruption" or violate the rights of others.

LEGALLY WED: Mildred and Richard Loving after the Supreme Court outlawed bans on interracial marriage.

The Right to Love

A 1967 Supreme Court case made interracial marriages legal across the country.

The sheriff and his men came about 2 a.m. Richard Loving heard the knocking, but before he could get out of bed, the officers broke through the door and burst into the bedroom. Later, Mildred Loving recalled the sudden panic, the flashlights in her face.

"They asked Richard who [I was]. I said, 'I'm his wife.' The sheriff said, 'Not around here you're not.'"

The place was rural Caroline County, Virginia, in July 1958. Richard, who was white, and Mildred, who was black and Native American, had committed a crime. They had violated Virginia's Racial Integrity Act, which made it "unlawful for any white person in this State to marry [anyone except] a white person."

For their offense, the Lovings were nearly sent to prison and then banished from Virginia. But they fought back in court. In the end, the Supreme Court ruled in their favor,

ILLEGAL IN 16 STATES:
Mildred and Richard Loving at home in Virginia

erasing 16 state laws that banned interracial marriage. A half-century later, *Loving v. Virginia* continues to help protect the right of Americans to marry anyone they want.

Race, Marriage, and the Law

By the time the Lovings were arrested, nearly a century had passed since the 14th Amendment to the Constitution (1868) guaranteed "equal protection of the laws" to all citizens regardless of race. Yet black people still faced many barriers to equality in the U.S.

This was especially true in the former slaveholding states of the South. There, Jim Crow laws and practices protected the dominance and "racial purity" of whites. For example, even after the Supreme Court outlawed racially segregated public schools in 1954 with *Brown v. Board of Education* (see p. 89), many of the South's schools were still segregated.

Yet in places like Caroline County, the lives of blacks and whites were intertwined. "[My parents] grew up within three or four miles of each other," Richard and Mildred's daughter, Peggy Loving, said in a 2011 documentary about the case. Black and white families routinely helped each other harvest their crops. In that small world, it wasn't so incredible that Mildred Jeter and Richard Loving would meet and fall in love.

"People had been mixing all the time, so I didn't know any different," Mildred would later say. "I didn't know there was a law against it."

Even so, Richard and Mildred knew some people in their community still felt threatened by racial mixing. When they wed in June 1958, they did it quietly in Washington, D.C. About five weeks later, they were arrested back home.

Brought before Judge Leon Bazile in January 1959, the Lovings feared being convicted and thrown in prison. So they pleaded guilty in exchange for a one-year sentence. Bazile then suspended the sentence, meaning that the Lovings wouldn't have to go to prison, but only if they agreed to his terms: They would have to leave Virginia for 25 years. If they returned together, they'd have to do the time.

The Civil Rights Movement Changes America

Mildred and Richard decided to leave Virginia. They moved to Washington, D.C., but they struggled to adjust to the city. Often, they would sneak back to Virginia.

Meanwhile, the world was changing. The civil rights movement and protests against racial segregation, many led by Martin Luther King Jr., filled the news. In early 1963, Mildred wrote to Attorney General Robert Kennedy explaining their situation. Kennedy referred them to the American Civil Liberties Union (ACLU), an organization that represents clients in civil rights cases. There, Mildred's letter reached the desk of a young lawyer named Bernard Cohen.

He knew the case would likely take years to resolve and might well go all the way to the Supreme Court. Cohen also believed the chances of winning were high—and made better by the plaintiffs' last name. "It was a very good omen," he said.

A vast majority of Americans now approve of interracial marriage.

"God . . . Did Not Intend for the Races to Mix"

First, Cohen appealed to Judge Bazile to reconsider the case. Bazile's decision, in January 1965, showed them what they were up against.

"Almighty God created the races white, black, yellow . . . and red, and he placed them on separate continents," Bazile stated. "The fact that he separated the races shows that he did not intend for the races to mix."

Cohen appealed the case through state and federal courts. Finally, in April 1967, *Loving v. Virginia* reached the U.S. Supreme Court. Cohen asked Richard if there was anything he wanted the justices of the Supreme Court to know.

"Tell the court I love my wife, and it is just unfair that I can't live with her in Virginia," Richard said.

Two months later, on June 12, the court unanimously backed the Lovings, ruling 9–0 that Virginia's law violated the 14th Amendment. Said Chief Justice Earl Warren: "Under our Constitution, the freedom to marry . . . a person of another race resides with the individual and cannot be infringed by the State."

For the Lovings, things were simpler. "I feel free now," Richard said.

The Impact of Freedom to Marry

The decision had an immediate effect, allowing interracial couples to get married in any state. But social attitudes still had catching up to do. According to a 1968 Gallup poll, 73 percent of Americans disapproved of interracial marriage.

Yet the case helped bring about profound changes in society. By 2013, 87 percent of Americans approved of interracial marriage. That same year, the Pew Research Center reported, a record high of 12 percent of American newlyweds were interracial couples.

Then, in 2015, the Supreme Court returned to the case in a 5–4 decision (*Obergefell V. Hodges*; see p. 89) that struck down state laws against same-sex marriage. Justice Anthony Kennedy cited Loving to insist that marrying whoever one chooses was one of the "fundamental liberties" protected by the Constitution.

The impact of the Loving case is perhaps best illustrated by the generations of people who have been able to marry over the past 50 years. "So many children and couples . . . are products of that ruling," says Nancy Buirski, director of the documentary *The Loving Story*.

By fighting for their marriage, the Lovings made history. As Peggy Loving has said of her parents: "I believe that's what they were put here on Earth to do." ■

The Impact of a Supreme Court Ruling

The Supreme Court in Washington, D.C., is the ultimate judge of all laws and the decisions of lower courts that come before it. The nine justices of the Supreme Court have the power to decide which of those laws or decisions are constitutional, meaning they are consistent with the Constitution.

A Supreme Court decision can have a sweeping impact. In the case of *Loving v. Virginia*, when the justices ruled that Virginia's law against interracial marriage was unconstitutional, 15 similar state laws were struck down at the same time.

Longest-Serving Justice
Clarence Thomas, since 1991

Oldest Justice
Ruth Bader Ginsburg, born 1933

Newest Justice
Brett Kavanaugh, since 2019

Youngest Justice
Neil Gorsuch, born 1967

Should Supreme Court Justices Serve for Life?

Like all federal judges, the nine justices of the Supreme Court serve for life, as specified in the Constitution. The Framers wanted the justices to be able to do their work without worrying about politics and the need to get re-elected.

Seats on the court normally open up when a justice resigns, retires, or dies. When a vacancy on the court occurs, the president nominates a replacement, who must then be approved by the Senate.

Since the Supreme Court was established in 1789, only 114 people have served on the court. The longest-serving justice was on the court for 36 years; of the current nine justices, Clarence Thomas, who joined the court in 1991, is the longest-serving; the oldest, in her late 80s, is Ruth Bader Ginsburg.

As justices age, no one knows which president will get the chance to nominate their replacements and what that will do to the balance of the court.

Turn the page to see how the two sides present their arguments in this debate. ➜

DEBATE

Ideally, the best legal minds in the nation sit on the Supreme Court. Why would we want to cut short their time on the court and lose the benefit of their experience in interpreting the Constitution?

When there is a vacancy on the nine-member court, the president nominates a replacement. Because presidential appointments must be approved by the Senate, the justices are very well-vetted by the time they take their seats on the court.

More importantly, with life tenure, the justices have complete freedom to judge the cases that come before them without worrying about the political pressures that the president and members of Congress face: They don't have to run for re-election or worry about criticism in the press or social media. Life tenure gives the justices the freedom to examine every case on its own merits and rule according to the constitutional principles they have sworn to uphold.

Some people advocate fixed terms for the justices, so everyone would know in advance how long they would serve on the court. Others are concerned about the advanced ages of some of the justices.

There is no reason to strip justices of their tenure based on age: Some of the most revered and hard-working Supreme Court justices served into their 80s and 90s. For example, John Paul Stevens was 90 years old when he retired in 2010, after 35 productive years on the Supreme Court.

Forced retirements, either on the basis of age or term limits, would in many cases mean losing outstanding members of the court. And with that loss comes the loss of valuable experience—sometimes decades of hearing and deciding cases dealing with a wide range of constitutional issues. We simply can't afford that as a nation. ■

> **Forced retirements, either on the basis of age or term limits, would mean losing many outstanding members of the Supreme Court.**

DEBATE POINTS

★ With lifetime appointments, justices are not subject to the political pressures the executive and legislative branches face.
★ Some of the most revered justices served for decades and into advanced age.
★ Limiting time on the court would deprive it of the experience of long-serving justices.

NO **Lifetime appointments are incompatible with one of the guiding principles of American democracy:** governance by the people and for the people. The Supreme Court determines the law of the land, so it should include a greater number and diversity of voices, which is difficult to achieve with the low turnover rate that results from lifetime appointments to the court.

Setting term limits on the Supreme Court—even generous ones of 15 or 20 years—would give justices plenty of time to make their mark on the court. However, it would also prevent justices from staying too long, particularly as they age out of their best and most productive years. It's simply bad policy to have justices writing decisions from hospital beds or when experiencing mental decline.

The importance of these nine positions requires that they be filled with the best legal minds in America. As justices sit on the court for decades, they can become rigid in their thinking, while new, open-minded justices would bring fresh perspectives to the issues of the day. According to the *New York Times*, in 1983, before he became a judge, Chief Justice John Roberts considered "setting a term of, say, 15 years [which] would ensure that federal judges would not lose all touch with reality through decades of ivory tower existence."

Currently, justices hold their seats until either death or retirement. Some try to time their retirements for when there's a president who will nominate a replacement with views similar to theirs.

Term limits would allow for fresh legal thinking and new perspectives on the key issues of the day.

Justices should not be putting off their retirement for the right political moment.

Nor should the resignation or death of a justice, or multiple justices, give a president so much power to determine the future of the court. Limiting terms of service for the justices would allow for a regular revitalization of the all-important Supreme Court. ■

DEBATE POINTS

★ Term limits would make it less likely that justices remain on the court when they're in ill health or no longer as productive.
★ Term limits would increase the low turnover rate and provide an opportunity for new legal thinking and perspectives on the court.
★ Term limits would reduce the arbitrary timing of replacements, which can give a single president the power to shape the court for decades.

Court Is in Session!

There are few places in Washington, D.C., as serious as the Supreme Court: The decisions of the nine justices really do impact the lives of millions of Americans for decades. But that doesn't stop the justices from occasionally cracking jokes from the bench, if only to break the tension. In fact, several justices are known to have pretty wicked senses of humor.

In any case, there's nothing to stop cartoonists from finding some humor in the court. Maybe in some cases the rulings don't come from intense research and study, the top cartoonist seems to (hopefully!) joke. In the bottom cartoon the court seems to have come up with a new way to announce their decisions. (In reality, one of the nine justices solemnly reads the court's decisions in the courtroom.) ■

Analyze the Cartoons

1. If you asked Supreme Court justices how they decide cases, what do think they would say?

2. How does that compare with what the justice in the top cartoon says?

3. How does the court announce its decisions in the bottom cartoon?

4. What does that say about how closely the public follows the court's rulings?

"Don't spread it around, but on the really tough ones, I just go with 'eenie, meenie, minie, moe.'"

PRESIDENT Barack Obama (2009–17), the 44th president, accompanies his successor, Donald Trump, the 45th, to his inauguration at the Capitol, January 20, 2017.

THE FIRST INAUGURATION, of George Washington in April 1789, took place in New York, then the nation's capital.

INAUGURATION DAY was March 4—four months after the election—until 1937, when the 20th Amendment moved it to January 20.

UNIT · 6
The Presidency

By 2020, the U.S. had had only 45 presidents.
Each man (no women so far) brought his own
strengths and weaknesses to the White House.

FIND MORE ONLINE: www.scholastic.com/howamericaworks

Is the Presidency an Impossible Job?

An inside look at what is probably the most powerful job in the world

Nobody said being president would be easy. The president leads the planet's strongest superpower. He or she commands a massive military and can tap huge financial resources with the stroke of a pen.

Yet when Donald Trump took office in 2017, other officials in the U.S. government didn't hesitate to say no to him. For example, Democrats in Congress blocked the president's plan to build a wall along the U.S.-Mexico border—at least temporarily. And in 2019, he was impeached by the House, and in 2020 he was put on trial in the Senate and **acquitted**. (See p. 116.)

Trump wasn't the only president who has struggled with the limits of his power. Every president going back to George Washington (1789–97) has as well. That's how the Framers of the Constitution planned it. They organized the federal government so that each of its three branches—the executive branch (headed by the president), the legislative branch (Congress), and the judicial branch (the courts)—would have limited power. It was accomplished through a system of checks and balances. This system gives each of the three branches some measure of control, or at least influence, over the other two.

Something else unites our presidents: Almost all have found the responsibilities were much bigger and tougher than they expected. Many experts have called the presidency an impossible job.

Most of the president's basic responsibilities are outlined in the Constitution. Others were created by acts of Congress or through tradition.

Here's a look at the seven main roles of our nation's highest elected official.

The U.S. Constitution outlines only the basics of a president's job today.

1. Commander in Chief

The Constitution divides the power to make war between the president and Congress. Only Congress can actually declare war on another country. But the Constitution names the president as commander in chief of the nation's armed forces.

That means the president decides where and when troops will be deployed, and how the U.S. will use its weapons. The commander in chief also has what's often called the "awesome responsibility" of deciding whether to attack a foreign country or even use nuclear weapons. President Harry S. Truman (1945–53) made that decision in April 1945 when he ordered atomic bombs to be dropped on two Japanese cities, Hiroshima and Nagasaki, to help end World War II (1939–45). Seventy-five years later, no other president has used nuclear weapons.

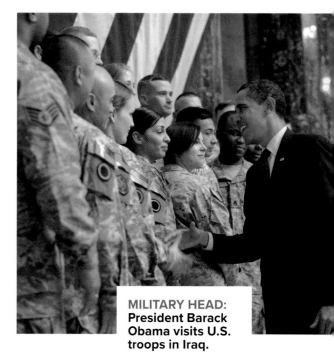

MILITARY HEAD: President Barack Obama visits U.S. troops in Iraq.

2. Head of the Executive Branch

The president oversees the entire federal government. Think of the president as the boss of one of the world's biggest companies. (Including the military, the U.S. government has more than 4 million employees!)

IN THE OVAL OFFICE:
John F. Kennedy
(1961–63) meets with
an important visitor,
his son, John Jr.

To keep the government running, each president chooses a group of top advisers called the cabinet. They supervise government departments including Defense (which oversees the armed forces), Transportation, and Education. George Washington's first cabinet had four people. As of 2020, President Trump had 23 people in his cabinet—including the director of homeland security and the attorney general.

Although laws are passed by Congress, it's the president's job to implement them. That's where the cabinet secretaries and the thousands of employees, taking direction from the president, come in.

The president also appoints federal judges—including to the nine-member Supreme Court. The president's nominees for both judges and cabinet members must be approved by the Senate.

One of a president's most important roles is to lead the nation in times of a crisis, whether a war, the coronavirus outbreak, or a severe economic downturn. It's up the president to get the machinery of government to respond, and to inspire the nation to persevere.

VROOM: President George W. Bush (2001–09) visits a Harley-Davidson factory in Pennsylvania.

3. Trying to Guide the Economy

The president shares responsibility for the economy with Congress and the private sector. But as chief executive, he or she is expected to help keep it running smoothly, trying to keep the unemployment rate down, help business create jobs, and keep inflation (increases in prices) as low as possible.

Every year, the president proposes a budget for the nation. This determines how much money each part of the government, such as the military, gets to spend. Congress then adds its priorities. The final budget must be passed by Congress and signed by the president. In 2019, the federal government's budget was $4.5 trillion. (That's $4,500,000,000,000!)

4. Head of State

As the head of state, the president acts as the symbol of the country. When the president welcomes foreign leaders or Super Bowl champions to the White House, he or she is representing the nation. Americans look to the president, especially in the nation's dealings with foreign leaders. The president's actions are expected to represent America's highest ideals and commitment to democracy.

5. Political Party Leader

The president serves as the leader of his or her political party and plays a key role in shaping its positions on issues. Presidents help raise money for their party and campaign for members who are running for office.

6. Head of Foreign Policy

The president sets the tone of America's relationships with other countries. He or she meets with foreign leaders, both in the U.S. and on trips abroad, and negotiates with them on tough issues. Chief among President Trump's foreign policy challenges are dealing with the nuclear weapons programs of North Korea and Iran, both of which are hostile to the U.S.

The president has the power to negotiate treaties—formal agreements with other countries that can promote trade or end wars. Before such agreements can take effect, however, they have to be ratified by the Senate.

7. Legislative Leader

Only Congress has the power to pass laws, but the president has to sign them to take effect. Presidents have many ways to influence legislation, including meeting with or calling members of the Senate or House to urge them to vote for or against particular bills.

And if a president disagrees with legislation passed by Congress, he can veto (reject) it. Congress can then try to override the president's veto with a two-thirds vote of both the House of Representatives and the Senate. ■

The commander in chief has to be ready to make life or death decisions about war and peace.

DONALD TRUMP (2017–) meets with North Korean leader Kim Jong Un.

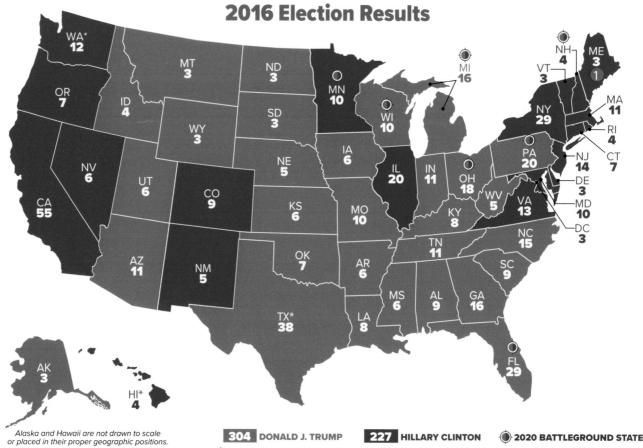

2016 Election Results

| WA* 12 | MT 3 | ND 3 | MN 10 | MI 16 | NH 4 | ME 3 / 1 | VT 3 | NY 29 | MA 11 |

Alaska and Hawaii are not drawn to scale or placed in their proper geographic positions.

304 DONALD J. TRUMP   **227** HILLARY CLINTON   ⊚ **2020 BATTLEGROUND STATE**

*Seven "faithless electors"—four from Washington State and one from Hawaii pledged to Clinton, and two from Texas pledged to Trump—voted for other candidates.

Electoral College 101

Don't understand the Electoral College? You're not alone. In plain English, here's how it works.

What exactly is the Electoral College?

This college doesn't have fraternities, a football team, or even classes. It's just 538 people called electors from all 50 states and Washington, D.C. According to the Constitution, they're responsible for electing the president and vice president. The winner needs a majority—at least 270—of the 538 electoral votes to become president.

How did this system come about?

In 1787, when the Constitution was being drafted, the Framers didn't want the president and vice president to be chosen directly by the people. They felt they needed to protect the country from what they saw as a largely ill-informed populace. They also wanted to establish a role for the states in national elections—in line with the idea of a federalist system of government. The Electoral College was their answer.

The Framers envisioned the Electoral College as an elite group of men (there wasn't a female elector until 1916) who

SPLIT DECISION: Democrat Hillary Clinton won the popular vote in 2016, but Republican Donald Trump won the electoral vote—and the presidency.

could be trusted to choose the nation's leaders. In some states, electors were chosen by the legislatures; in others, by popular vote.

The system was also supposed to ensure that a candidate with overwhelming support in only one part of the country—which might allow him to win a majority of the popular vote nationally—wouldn't be elected against the will of the rest of the nation.

Today, each state's political parties nominate slates (lists) of electors who are pledged to support the party's candidates.

How many electoral votes does each state get?

The same number as its delegation in Congress: the number of seats it has in the House of Representatives (which is based on population), plus two for the Senate.

For example, Florida has 27 representatives in the House and two senators, so it has 29 electoral votes. The six states with the most electoral votes in 2020 are California (55), Texas (38), New York (29), Florida (29), Illinois (20), and Pennsylvania (20).

One reason the census every 10 years is so important is that it determines how many seats each state has in the House of Representatives, and therefore how many votes it gets in the Electoral College. (2020 is a census year.)

If these 538 electors choose the president, then what's Election Day about?

Technically, Americans won't be voting for the Republican and Democratic (and other parties') nominees for president, even though their names will be on the ballot. They'll be voting for Democratic or Republican electors who are selected by each state's parties.

So how does a candidate win?

With the exception of Maine and Nebraska*, each state's electoral votes are awarded on a winner-take-all basis: The candidate with the most popular votes in a state—whether the margin of victory is 3 votes or 3 million votes—gets all of that state's electoral votes.

Do electors actually cast their votes?

It's usually a formality, but in mid-December, the electors representing the candidate who won their state's popular vote meet in their state capital and cast their votes.

The results become official when the states' electoral ballots are counted before a joint session of Congress on January 6. The winners are sworn in on Inauguration Day, January 20.

IN 2016 Democra[t] Hillary Clinton an[d] Republican Dona[ld] Trump battled ov[er] key states in the Electoral College like Ohio and Pennsylvania.

* According to the Constitution, each state decides how its electoral votes are allocated. Maine and Nebraska are the only two states in which the electoral votes can be split up depending how on the candidates do.

What if no candidate gets a 270-vote majority of the 538 electoral votes?

In that case, the Constitution says that the House elects the president from the three candidates with the most electoral votes. Each state gets one vote. The Senate elects the vice president from the two candidates with the most electoral votes, with each senator getting one vote.

Can one candidate win the popular vote and another win the electoral vote?

Yes, and the electoral vote determines who will be president. It happened in 2016, when Democrat Hillary Clinton won 66 million popular votes to Republican Donald Trump's 63 million. But Trump won 304 electoral votes to Clinton's 227—and the presidency. This Electoral College/popular vote split has happened four other times: in 1824, 1876, 1888, and 2000.

How does this split happen? In 2016, Clinton racked up huge margins in several high-population states like California and New York, but the big margins didn't help her. Trump won some key states like Wisconsin by very small popular-vote margins. But again, the margin doesn't matter: He still got all of those states' electoral votes, and the electoral votes are what put him in the White House.

How has this played out in recent elections?

Candidates don't spend much time, or TV and internet ad dollars, in states where they're way behind or way ahead. Instead, they target "battleground states" that look close. In the last few elections, 5 to 10 states (see map on p. 110) were considered up for grabs and critical to an Electoral College victory.

That means if you live in states like California and Massachusetts, which tend to vote Democratic, or Alaska and Mississippi, which tend to vote Republican, you're probably not going to get too many visits from the candidates or see a lot of their ads.

On the other hand, if you live in battleground states like Wisconsin, Ohio, or Florida, it may feel like the candidates have moved into your living room and taken over your TV, computer screens, and phone. ■

The Electoral College is why Wisconsin, Ohio, and Florida get so much attention in presidential races today.

IMPEACHED AND ACQUITTED: Speaker of the House Nancy Pelosi led the effort to impeach President Donald Trump.

How Impeachment Works

The Constitution provides only three ways to remove a president from office: the ballot box, term limits, and impeachment.

"The President, Vice President and all civil Officers of the United States, shall be removed from Office on Impeachment for, and Conviction of, Treason, Bribery, or other high Crimes and Misdemeanors."

—U.S. Constitution, Article II, Section 4

The Framers made the constitutional process for trying to remove a president from office, known as impeachment, intentionally difficult. Here's how it works:

1. What is impeachment?

As part of the system of checks and balances, the Constitution permits Congress to remove presidents before their term is up if they're found to have committed "treason, bribery, or other high crimes and misdemeanors." Impeachment is the first step in that process. The Framers established impeachment as a safeguard against presidents abusing their office.

Having just fought for independence from the tyranny of King George III of Britain, the Founders worried about presidents becoming too powerful. They divided the federal government into three branches—executive, legislative, and judicial—that have the ability to check one another's power. They gave the legislature, and specifically the House of Representatives, "the sole power of impeachment."

The Constitution doesn't say what "high crimes and misdemeanors" means.

2. What are "high crimes and misdemeanors"?

There's no easy answer because the Constitution doesn't actually say. The Framers specifically mentioned treason and bribery as impeachable offenses but didn't list the "other high crimes and misdemeanors." Constitutional scholars still debate the phrase's meaning. Most say it means a serious abuse of power or misconduct in office. It doesn't necessarily mean that a specific law was broken.

3. What is the process?

Generally, a committee in the House of Representatives will investigate the president for alleged offenses. They'll call on witnesses to appear before them, and they'll ask for documents.

If the committee determines there's enough evidence of wrongdoing, they'll bring formal charges, known as articles of impeachment, to the full House. The House would then hold a vote on one or more of the articles. If at least one article gets a majority (218 votes out of 435), the president would be impeached.

4. What happens if the House votes to impeach?

When a president is impeached, he or she has essentially been charged with crimes, and like anyone else in America, is entitled to a trial.

That trial is held in the Senate and presided over by the chief justice of the Supreme Court. A team of lawmakers from the House, known as impeachment managers, play the role of prosecutors, presenting the case against the president. The president has defense lawyers, and the senators serve as the jury.

If at least two-thirds of the senators (67 of 100) find the president guilty on any of the articles, he or she is removed from office, and the vice president takes over as president.

That has never happened. Three presidents have been impeached by the House—Andrew Johnson in 1868, Bill Clinton in 1998, and Donald Trump in 2019. All three were acquitted by the Senate and were able to continue in office.

In the case of Richard Nixon in 1974, when it became clear that there was enough support in Congress to impeach him and remove him from office, he resigned.

5. Can anyone else be impeached?

Yes. The Constitution says that not only the president, but also the "Vice President and all civil Officers of the United States" (in other words, all federal officials) can be impeached and removed from office.

In addition to three presidents, 17 other officials have been impeached since 1788, including senators, federal judges, Supreme Court justices, and a cabinet secretary. In 2010, Judge G. Thomas Porteous Jr. of Louisiana was impeached and found guilty and removed from office by the Senate. The four articles of impeachment included charges that he had received cash and favors from lawyers who had dealings in his court. ■

ONLY FOUR PRESIDENTS HAVE FACED IMPEACHMENT
One resigned; the other three survived their trials in the Senate.

Andrew Johnson, 1868
President Abraham Lincoln's vice president and successor was impeached for violating a law that was later ruled unconstitutional. The Senate vote was one short of what was needed to remove him from office.

Bill Clinton, 1998
Clinton became the second U.S. president to be impeached after lying under oath about his relationship with a 22-year-old White House intern. He was acquitted by the Senate.

Richard Nixon, 1974
Nixon resigned to avoid impeachment and removal from office. A burglary at Democratic Party offices in the Watergate building in Washington had revealed abuses of power by his administration and efforts to cover them up.

Donald Trump, 2019
Trump was impeached for trying to get the European nation of Ukraine to investigate a political opponent, presidential candidate and former vice president Joe Biden (2009–17). He was acquitted after a Senate trial in early 2020.

Should We Elect the President by Popular Vote?

When the Framers drafted the Constitution in 1787, they thought that average citizens weren't educated enough to elect the president. That's why they created an indirect system called the Electoral College.

The Electoral College is a group of 538 people from all 50 states and Washington, D.C., called electors. A candidate must win a majority (270) of the 538 electoral votes to become president.* (See p. 110.)

Each state has a number of electors equal to its total number of senators and representatives. For example, Texas has 36 representatives in the House and two senators, so it has 38 electors. Since representation in the House is based on population, states with more people have more electors.

More than 230 years after the Constitution was adopted, many Americans want to abolish the Electoral College and elect the president by popular vote. Others say the Electoral College has served the nation well and see no reason to change it.

* Electors are supposed to vote for the candidates their state voted for, but in a few cases they haven't. In early 2020, the Supreme Court heard two cases about what are known as "faithless electors."

Turn the page to see how the two sides present their arguments in this debate. →

DEBATE

YES The way we elect the president should reflect America's democratic values. But two of the last four presidents made it to the White House without winning a majority of votes—known as the popular vote. They won only the most electoral votes.

"In fact, the second-place candidate has been elected four** times, most recently in 2016," says John R. Koza, the chair of National Popular Vote, which is working to replace the Electoral College with the popular vote.

"Donald Trump won 304 electoral votes, and the presidency," Koza notes, "despite receiving almost 3 million fewer popular votes than his opponent, Hillary Clinton."

The Electoral College is a relic of a time when most people didn't have access to information about the candidates. It was also an effort by the Framers to give smaller and more rural states more power than their populations warranted.

Today the Electoral College forces candidates to focus their attention almost exclusively on swing, or battleground, states, which "swing" back and forth between the parties.

For candidates, it's perfectly logical: Why spend time and ad dollars in states like reliably Democratic Illinois or reliably Republican Indiana, if the outcome is virtually certain, and the popular vote margin doesn't make any difference?

That makes millions of voters in non-battleground states like California and Alabama feel their votes don't matter.

But if you're in a swing state like Wisconsin, Ohio, or Florida, you may feel as if the candidates have taken over your TV and phone with their ads. Getting rid of the Electoral College would make every vote count and motivate more people to vote.

The Electoral College encourages candidates to focus on undecided voters in a few key battleground states instead of trying to gain the support of undecided voters nationally. That means most states, and most voters, are ignored. ∎

Our current system means that voters in most states are virtually ignored.

DEBATE POINTS

★ The Electoral College can award the presidency to a candidate with millions fewer votes than his or her opponent.
★ The Electoral College forces candidates to spend all their time in a few key swing, or battleground, states, ignoring the vast majority of the American people.
★ Relying on the popular vote would give all voters, regardless of their state, equal representation and more motivation to vote.

In addition to Donald Trump in 2016, the other three were George W. Bush in 2000; Benjamin Harrison in 1888; and Rutherford B. Hayes in 1876.

 **The Electoral College has been the law of the land for over 230 years.** The Framers created this system to make sure that smaller and more rural states had a real voice, and that the election process wasn't dominated by big states and cities.

"There have been more than 700 attempts to amend the Constitution to abolish the Electoral College; all have failed," explains Robert Hardaway, author of *The Electoral College and the Constitution*.

The latest attempt to change the system is the National Popular Vote plan. It would work around the Electoral College, instead of trying to actually abolish it, which would take a constitutional amendment.

Under the National Popular Vote plan, states would agree in advance to award their electoral votes to the winner of the national popular vote. This is possible because the Constitution gives the states the power to decide how their electoral votes are allocated.

Fifteen states and the District of Columbia (representing 196 of the 270 electoral votes needed to win the presidency) have endorsed the plan.

Getting rid of the Electoral College, or changing the way it works with something like the National Popular Vote plan, would affect our entire political process. It would encourage smaller parties and fringe candidates to run nationwide and further splinter the vote. That would make it harder for the winner to secure a large majority, which makes it easier to govern.

The Electoral College also prevents a few states or cities with the largest populations determining the winner. And because no single region has enough electoral votes to secure a 270-vote majority, the Electoral College requires a president to have support from voters across the country. This helps ensure that he or she will address the concerns of America's increasingly diverse population. ∎

The Electoral College helps ensure that support for a president is broad as well as deep.

DEBATE POINTS

★ **The Electoral College ensures that the president has support from different parts of the country.**

★ **Big cities and states alone should not determine the winner, which could happen if we used the popular vote.**

★ **Changing the Electoral College would threaten the two-party system and make it harder for the winner to gain a large majority of the vote.**

Would You Want This Job?!?!

The United States has had only one president—Ronald Reagan (1981–89)—who was a professional actor before he went into politics. But the reality is all presidents, and presidential candidates, have to do some acting, or at least posturing.

Take a look at the top cartoon from the 1912 presidential campaign, which pitted former president Theodore Roosevelt (in the cowboy hat) and Governor Woodrow Wilson of New Jersey (in the cap) against President William Howard Taft (in the top hat). Who's doing the acting here? (Wilson won, by the way.)

In the bottom cartoon you'll see President Ulysses S. Grant. He led the Union Army to victory in the Civil War (1861–65) before he became president. How does he look to you after shouldering the burden of the presidency? ■

Analyze the Cartoons

1. How are the presidential candidates in the top cartoon acting? How does that compare to how the cartoonist thinks they are actually feeling?

2. Why do you think presidents and presidential candidates need to do some acting, or at least some posturing?

3. What are a few of the burdens that President Grant is bearing in the bottom cartoon?

4. If you drew a cartoon of a 21st-century president—say, Donald Trump or his predecessor, Barack Obama—what burdens would you show them dealing with?

Why Voting Matters

In 2018, a race for a seat in the Virginia legislature ended in a tie. To determine the winner, election officials put the candidates' names in a bowl and held a blind drawing.

VIRGINIA TIEBREAKER: All **23,216 votes** really counted!

ELECTIONS sometimes come down to a difference of just a few votes.

It's True: *Every* Vote Counts

In 2018, Virginians watched as an important election was decided in an unusual way: An election official reached into a bowl, pulled out a name, and announced the winner.

The drawing was the culmination of a two-month battle in a neck-and-neck race between Republican incumbent David Yancey and Democratic challenger Shelly Simonds for a seat in the Virginia House of Delegates. After a recount and a court ruling, the two candidates found themselves with 11,608 votes each. And according to Virginia law, tied elections must be settled by "lot," or a drawing. Yancey's name was picked.

Pulling names out of a bowl may sound strange, but the results of the tiebreaker had serious consequences. In determining the winner of the race, more was at stake than just one seat—party control of the Virginia House was on the line.

Yancey's win allowed Republicans to maintain a narrow 51–49 majority in the House—crucial to the party after a recent wave of Democratic wins. The nail-biter of a race was a reminder, says political analyst Quentin Kidd of Christopher Newport University in Virginia, that just one vote can determine an election's outcome.

"I've never had as many conversations with people who are thankful that they voted—or are really upset that they didn't—than I've had since this particular tied election," Kidd says of the Virginia race.

"It really does drive home the [idea] that every vote counts."

2000 Presidential Election

For many Americans, Virginia's election cliff-hanger brought back memories of the 2000 U.S. presidential election. That famous race—between Republican George W. Bush and Democrat Al Gore—came down to a difference of just 537 votes in Florida and was ultimately decided by the Supreme Court. (The court ruled in favor of Bush.)

A first count of ballots in Virginia showed that Yancey had won by 10 votes out of the more than 23,000 cast. But Simonds asked for a recount. And in the second count, she gained 11 votes—making her the winner by one vote.

But the next day, a three-judge panel, after reviewing the recount, allowed an additional, contested ballot to be counted for Yancey. The ballot in question had the names filled in for both candidates but a slash mark through Simonds's name. The race was declared dead even—and in January 2018 Virginia held its first election tiebreaker in decades.

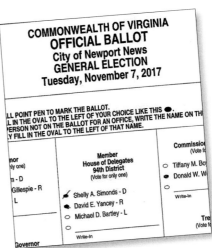

THE CONTESTED ballot that tied the race—and led to the tiebreaker

Tiebreaker vs. Redo

A drawing may seem like a random way of deciding an election, but Kidd says it's a fair way to break ties.

"Some people might argue that an [election] redo would make more sense, but you would end up getting people who didn't vote the first time voting in the second race," Kidd says. "That seems less fair than simply breaking the tie by chance."

And the Winner Is . . .

Here's how other states have settled deadlocked elections.

DRAW STRAWS

To break a tied race—4,589 votes apiece—for a seat in the Mississippi House in 2015, candidates drew straws. The Democrat chose the longer straw, making him the winner.

HIGH CARD WINS

In a tied race of 107 votes each for a Nevada county seat in 2002, candidates chose cards. Both picked jacks, but the Democrat's spade beat his opponent's diamond.

NAMES OUT OF A HAT

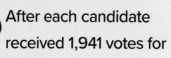

After each candidate received 1,941 votes for a Wyoming House seat in 1994, the Republican eventually won when his name was pulled from a cowboy hat.

In fact, choosing public officials by drawing has a long history. In ancient Greece, officeholders were selected at random from a pool of candidates. And in 14th-century Italy, officials were chosen from names drawn out of a sack. The U.S. has also had its share of tied elections—and unique ways of breaking them (See "And the Winner Is . . ." at left.)

An "Amazing Civics Lesson"

In Virginia, Simonds conceded, but ran again in 2019 and won.

"We've had an amazing civics lesson in the power of every vote," she said after the tiebreaker.

Looking ahead, memories of the Virginia tiebreaker may inspire more people to turn out at the polls. "Voting is your job as a citizen," Kidd says. "Had more people done their job [in Virginia], their candidate may have won, and this race may not have been a tie." ■

OFFERING A FLOWER to troops guarding the Pentagon, America's military headquarters, during a **1968** protest against the Vietnam War

1971: 18-Year-Olds Get the Vote

In 1971, at the height of the Vietnam War, the 26th Amendment lowered the voting age from 21 to 18.

Young people, especially college students, were at the forefront of the social and political changes that rocked America in the 1960s. Teens and 20-somethings participated in and led sit-ins, Freedom Rides, and marches demanding civil rights for black people, greater opportunities for women, and an end to the war in Vietnam.

But while they could march and shout and sign all the petitions they wanted, many protesters had no say in the election of the country's leaders, who could actually make the changes they were calling for. That's because although men were being drafted to fight at 18, the voting age in most of the country was 21.

That wouldn't change until 1971, when the 26th Amendment to the Constitution gave Americans the right to vote in any election at age 18. While there had been talk about lowering the voting age for decades, the idea didn't catch on until the turmoil of the 1960s.

"With the youth rebellion, women's rights and civil rights protests, and antiwar sentiment over the war in Vietnam, the whole culture lent itself to get 18-year-olds the vote," says Robert Langran of Villanova University in Pennsylvania.

The modern push for the 18-year-old vote actually began during World War II (1939–45), when Congress lowered the draft age from 21 to 18.

"If young men are to be drafted at 18 years of age to fight for their government," Senator Arthur Vandenberg of Michigan told the *New York Times* in 1942, "they ought to be entitled to vote at 18 years of age for the kind of government for which they are best satisfied to fight."

"GIVE ME LIBERTY OR GIVE ME DEATH": Patrick Henry's 1775 speech against British rule makes a comeback at a 1970 rally for the 26th Amendment.

Wars and Voting Rights

But that effort, and others that followed, went nowhere. Though politicians often said they favored lowering the voting age, most worried they would be driven from office by a groundswell of young voters—and they waited till their hand was forced by the upheaval surrounding the Vietnam War (1954–75) in the 1960s.

"Every shift in voting rights is associated with a war," says Alexander Keyssar, a professor at Harvard University in Massachusetts.

For African Americans, it was initially the Civil War (1861–65). For women, it was World War I (1914–18), when suffrage associations that contributed to the war effort brought visibility to their cause. For 18-year-olds, it was the Vietnam War, which the U.S. entered in the early 1960s and exited in 1975, with 58,000 Americans killed. College campuses across the U.S. became centers of antiwar protests, and the World War II cry of "old enough to fight, old enough to vote" was resurrected.

YOUNG PEOPLE argued that they should not be sent to fight in wars if they did not have a voice in government.

At first many disagreed. "The requirements for a good soldier and for a good voter are not the same," read a 1967 *New York Times* editorial. But by 1970 the tide had shifted, with the *Times* arguing that "suffrage for this group of Americans is a matter of simple justice."

In March 1971, in less than two weeks, Congress passed a constitutional amendment to lower the voting age to 18 in all elections. The wording was simple: "The right of citizens of the United States, who are eighteen years of age or older, to vote shall not be denied or abridged by the United States or by any State on account of age."

The Impact of Young Voters

Five states—Connecticut, Delaware, Minnesota, Tennessee, and Washington State—ratified the amendment that first day. And in just 100 days, a record time, 38 states were on board. On July 5, the 26th Amendment was certified. Suddenly, 10 million more Americans had the right to vote.

Republicans feared young voters would defeat President Richard Nixon (1969–74) in his 1972 re-election bid, and officials in college towns worried that students would vote them out. But most political scientists predicted little impact. "Some groups in American life vote **monolithically**," Richard Scammon, an expert on voting behavior, told the *Times*. "Young people don't."

In the 1972 presidential election, 18- to 24-year-olds were expected to turn out in large numbers, with most supporting the antiwar Democratic candidate, George McGovern. But only 52 percent voted, compared with 68 percent of voters 25 and older. Nixon was re-elected in a landslide. Since then, young voter turnout has generally been even lower. The percentage of young people voting in presidential elections has never again reached the 50 percent mark. However, in recent elections, more young people have been voting.

Young people could play a critical role in elections—if they vote. ∎

Has a "Youth Wave" Begun?

Youth turnout surged in 2018. Will young people take their interest in issues like climate change and gun violence to the ballot box?

Maddy Scannell, a 19-year-old sophomore at Rice University in Houston, not only voted for the first time in the 2018 midterm elections. She also spent hours every week registering fellow students to vote and educating them about the kind of paperwork and ID they would need to cast their ballots in Texas.

"I think the election was a referendum on the direction our country is heading," Scannell says about why she and other students got so involved.

Traditionally, young people have voted in lower proportions than every other age group. But in the 2018 midterm elections, the voter turnout rate for those ages 18 to 29 shot up to 36 percent, from 20 percent in the 2014 midterm elections.

That may not seem like a very high percentage, and it remains far below the 49 percent turnout for the electorate as a whole, but it sent a message, according to voting experts.

"It's huge," says Kei Kawashima-Ginsberg, director of civic engagement at CIRCLE, a group at Tufts University in Massachussets that tracks youth voting trends. "It's the highest turnout we've seen since we started collecting data in 1994."

Fed Up with Division

Experts say this "youth wave" at the polls was due to a number of factors: Many young people are fed up with divisive politics and voted to express their dissatisfaction. The school shooting in 2018 at Marjory Stoneman Douglas High School in Parkland, Florida, and the student activism that followed also encouraged many young people to vote.

If youth turnout levels continue to rise in the coming years, it could have major implications for our political system. For one thing, it could push candidates to pay more attention to young voters and the issues they care about, such as the environment, student debt, health care, and gun violence.

"There's been an assumption over time . . . that young people are not really worth talking to because they're so unreliable as voters," Kawashima-Ginsberg says.

The lesson of the 2018 election, she says, is that young voters can have a huge impact on who wins and politicians should work to earn their votes. In fact, exit polls indicated that young voters were crucial to the outcome of several statewide races.

Taylor Swift Effect?

Even before Election Day, there were signs that 2018 might be different. Survivors of the Parkland school shooting responded to the tragedy by launching a political movement, calling on young people to register to vote and support gun control.

And a month before the election, Taylor Swift's plea to her 112 million Instagram followers to register to vote had an impact: In the 24-hour period after her post, 65,000 people registered.

Young voters were crucial to the outcome of several statewide races in 2018.

Given how poor youth turnout has been historically, no one knows whether the burst of political enthusiasm among young people will continue—or deepen.

"Young people are encouraged by their own impact," Kawashima-Ginsberg says. "Politics is now cool, and I think that's huge in terms of how sustainable this level of energy is." ∎

ELECTED OFFICES have a range of minimum ages—and some are lower than you might think.

Teens Head to the Statehouse

Meet three young people who recently won election to their state legislatures.

n 2017, six teenagers announced they were running for governor of Kansas. At ages 16 and 17, they weren't even old enough to vote yet—but at the time, there was no minimum age requirement to become the state's chief executive.*

The teens knew success was unlikely.

*Kansas has since passed a law that candidates must be at least 25 years old.

"The day a 17-year-old wins governor of any state will be the day pigs fly," Joseph Tutera Jr., one of the candidates, said during the campaign. But "Hey, we're here, we've got ideas."

Although none of the boys ended up winning, the race was evidence of a growing movement of young people who want a say in deciding issues that affect their lives, such as climate change, minimum-wage rates, and gun violence. In 2018, more teens began campaigning for seats in their state and local governments—and several won. "My generation wants to be part of solving the issues," says Kalan Haywood, who was elected at age 19 to the Wisconsin State Assembly. "Politics has been made cool."

These three lawmakers won their state races as teens in 2018:

CALEB HANNA
AGE AT ELECTION: 19

West Virginia House of Delegates

Hometown: Richwood, West Virginia

Party: Republican

On election night in 2018, Caleb Hanna sat with his parents in a McDonald's, anxiously awaiting election results. The 19-year-old had campaigned heavily for a seat in the West Virginia House

of Delegates, knocking on hundreds of doors in an attempt to reach every Republican who lived in his district. The odds were seemingly against him—but by 10:30 that night, Hanna learned he had toppled the Democratic incumbent by 25 percentage points. He celebrated with a burger and fries.

Hanna first became interested in politics when Barack Obama won the White House in 2008. Like many African Americans, he recalls his excitement at seeing "someone who looks like me become president." But he soon soured on Obama's policies; by 2012, he was a Mitt Romney fan.

In high school, Hanna tested out politics by serving first as class president and then as president of the student body.

As a Republican in the state capital, he planned to concentrate on education. For starters, he wanted to introduce a technical course that will prepare middle schoolers for future careers. "There are a lot of good-paying, high-skill jobs out there that don't require a four-year degree," he says. "We need to focus more on teaching kids about the opportunities in those fields."

In an era of tremendous partisanship, he also recognizes a need to work with Democrats. "It's the only way to make effective policy," Hanna says. "It's like pulling on a piece of taffy. They pull from one side of the table, and you pull on the other side."

CASSANDRA LEVESQUE
AGE AT ELECTION: 19
New Hampshire House of Representatives
Hometown: Barrington, New Hampshire
Party: Democratic

While working on a Girl Scout Gold Award project in 2016, Cassandra Levesque made a shocking discovery: New Hampshire, her home state, still allowed girls as young as 13 and boys as young as 14 to marry.

It took a lot of work, but Levesque eventually convinced New Hampshire's lawmakers to make a change. In 2018, Governor Chris Sununu signed a measure raising the state's marriage age to 16.

Thinking that was the end of it, Levesque went off to college to study photography. But when two seats in the state's House of Representatives opened up, local Democrats urged her to run.

Reluctant at first, she made a pros and cons list, and "all the cons started turning to pros," says Levesque, who recently turned 20. She filed to run on the next-to-last possible day.

Canvassing and attending local events as a candidate was scary at first. But she knew many people from growing up in town, and they were supportive of her on the campaign trail.

After being sworn into office, Levesque became a member of the Children and Family Law Committee, where she focuses on bills that help women and kids. She's committed to raising the marriage age to 18, as well as figuring out ways to bring young people back to the state. Her youthful perspective is especially important, she says, because the average age in the state legislature is 66.

"I haven't run into many people who think my age is discouraging," she says. "They're just excited that I'm there."

KALAN HAYWOOD

AGE AT ELECTION: 19

Wisconsin State Assembly

Hometown: Milwaukee, Wisconsin

Party: Democratic

The importance of Kalan Haywood's new role truly hit him when he first sat behind his desk in the state capitol. The young Democrat hadn't even been sworn in yet, but that didn't matter.

"All the responsibility, the full weight of the job sank in at that moment," he says. "I was like 'I want to start now.'"

By age 8, Haywood already knew he wanted to be a politician. At 13, he worked on his first political campaign, collecting signatures and putting up signs for a local lawmaker. A year later, he joined the Milwaukee Youth Council, eventually becoming its president.

Even with some political experience, running his campaign for the Wisconsin State Assembly was a "whole other level of stress." But he loved meeting so many diverse groups of people.

"That was one of the best experiences of my life," he says.

His priorities include education, economic development, public safety, and encouraging youth civic engagement.

"I want young people running for all levels of government—state, town, city—or being campaign managers or chiefs of staff," Haywood says. "I don't want to be the youngest in 2020." ■

Should the Voting Age Be Lowered?

n many states, 16-year-olds can drive or get a job, and must pay taxes on their wages. But there's one thing most of them aren't allowed to do: vote.

The 26th Amendment, ratified in 1971, lowered the voting age to 18 from 21. But while the amendment gives every American 18 or over the right to vote, it doesn't prevent cities or states from allowing younger people to vote in local elections. In fact, a few cities in Maryland already allow 16- and 17-year-olds to vote, and lawmakers in several states are considering lowering the voting age to 17.

Turn the page to see how the two sides present their arguments in this debate. →

 **YES** **Young student activists are raising their voices on issues like climate change and gun violence**. In fact, in the last few years, more 16- and 17-year-olds have become politically active on all fronts. Yet they cannot vote on issues that have a direct bearing on their lives and their futures.

In several countries, including Austria, Malta, Brazil, and Scotland, the voting age is 16. These young voters tend to vote at higher rates than their older peers.

"Considering that 18- to 24-year-olds have the lowest turnout of any age group in the U.S., allowing people to begin voting even younger—when they're more likely to cast ballots—might increase future turnout," according to Laurence Steinberg, a psychology professor at Temple University in Philadelphia, Pennsylvania.

"The current push to lower the voting age is motivated by outrage that those most vulnerable to school shootings have no say in how such atrocities are best prevented," he says. "Let's give those young people more than just their voices to make a change."

One of the rallying cries in 1776 was, "No taxation without representation." That same principle should apply today. Teens as young as 14 can work. How can we tax them if the workers get no say in their governance?

In a democracy, the people should be not only allowed but also encouraged to engage in government. We wait too long and lose those most driven to vote by denying them the right to do so. ■

In the last few years, more 16- and 17-year-olds have become politically active.

DEBATE POINTS

★ **Young people have the biggest stake in the future and should be encouraged to get politically involved as early as possible.**
★ **Lowering the voting age may help create more lifelong voters.**
★ **Teens as young as 14 are allowed to work and must pay taxes on their wages; they should have a say in how those taxes are spent.**

 **NO** **We of course want to have more young people involved in politics and invested in their government.** Teens, however, often lack a clear understanding of how our government works, and it's critical that voters of all ages be informed on both the issues of the day and how government works.

We are at a moment when there are some very politically active young people, which is a terrific thing for America. Still, most teens lack the understanding and maturity to politically engage. The developing brain is not fully formed until the mid-20s.

Instead of providing more privileges to those still developing rational thinking, we should provide more support to help them develop the skills and knowledge they need to become engaged citizens at 18.

Voting is a key civic responsibility. At 18, citizens are asked to serve on juries, and they can enlist in the armed forces. It follows that at this age they should also be granted the right to vote. While everyone must pay taxes, these other responsibilities are more in line with the power of voting.

David Davenport, a research fellow at the Hoover Institution in California, told NBC News, "My concern is if 16-year-olds were allowed to vote on any kind of broad scale, what we'd actually be doing is bringing the least politically informed, the least politically experienced, the least mature in terms of making long-term judgments and trade-offs, directly into and potentially affecting our voter turnout and results." ■

Most younger teens lack the maturity and the knowledge to be informed citizens.

DEBATE POINTS

★ **American teens do not as a group have a clear knowledge of the government and therefore cannot make informed decisions about it.**
★ **Voting in elections requires maturity that adolescents as a group do not have.**
★ **You need to be 18 to enlist in the military and serve on juries; it makes sense to get the right to vote at the same age.**

EDITORIAL CARTOONS

How Low Can You Go?

Voter turnout among young people (defined as voters from 18 to 29) has generally been low. In the 2018 midterm elections, however, their turnout shot up to 36 percent. (See p. 130.) What brought these young people to the polls? Probably a combination of strong feelings (both positive and negative) about President Donald Trump and issues like climate change and guns. That has some people thinking that the voting age should be even lower, so that today's more politically engaged high school students can have a say about issues that will affect them for the rest of their lives. But how low? Two cartoonists weigh in. ■

Analyze the Cartoons

1. Who's the man by the slide in the top political cartoon, and what's he doing in a playground?

2. What do you think the cartoonist is saying about efforts to lower the voting age?

3. At what age do you think people should be allowed to vote? Why?

4. In the bottom cartoon, what's going on in the two panels?

5. The cartoon's headline is "2 Good Ways to Get Lawmakers' Attention." How do you think the cartoonist feels about the two ways the cartoon depicts?

A SEGREGATED drinking fountain outside a county courthouse in Halifax, North Carolina, in 1938

COLORED

"COLORED," once used to describe African Americans, is now considered out-of-date and offensive.

ACROSS THE SOUTH, public facilities—from drinking fountains and restrooms to movie theaters and schools—were segregated.

SEGREGATION of public facilities was outlawed by the Civil Rights Act of 1964 and other legislation.

UNIT · 8

The Long Struggle for Civil Rights

The fight has gone on for centuries—and continues today.

A POLICE OFFICER threw Elizabeth Jennings off a New York streetcar in 1854. But she refused to let the incident pass.

The Civil Rights Hero You've Never Heard Of

A century before Rosa Parks, a black woman in New York refused to get off a whites-only streetcar, striking an early blow for equal rights.

t's a story that most Americans know well: In a city where black people suffer the daily humiliation of segregation, an African American woman stands her ground. One day, she defies the rules that separate blacks from whites on public transportation. Her act of resistance leads to changing those rules for good.

Who was that woman? Most would say Rosa Parks of Montgomery, Alabama. In 1955, her refusal to give up her bus seat to a white person led to a campaign to desegregate Montgomery's buses and helped spark the civil rights movement of the 1950s and '60s.

But this drama took place in New York City a century before Parks's protest. There, in 1854, 27-year-old Elizabeth Jennings refused a conductor's order to get off a streetcar with white passengers. After she was forced off, she sued the streetcar company and won.

You may not have heard of Elizabeth Jennings. Yet "her case was the one that helped break the back of segregation in New York," says Amy Hill Hearth, the author of a book about Jennings called *Streetcar to Justice.* Historians call Elizabeth Jennings one of America's first civil rights heroes.

Jennings's struggle foreshadowed the civil rights movement.

Free but Segregated New York

By 1804, laws had been passed to abolish slavery throughout the North, including in New York in 1799. In New York City, freedom had allowed a small but thriving black middle class to grow. Its leaders stressed self-improvement and strove to prove themselves equal to whites. Among the community's most prominent members was Thomas Jennings. A successful tailor, Jennings was the first African American to hold a U.S. patent, for an early method of dry-cleaning clothes. His daughter Elizabeth was a teacher.

Still, being free didn't mean being equal. "Black New Yorkers were second-class citizens," Hearth says. "Segregation was a way of life." Even successful black people faced limitations on where they could live, work, and mix with white people in public.

Most of those limitations were based on custom rather than actual laws. The city's streetcar lines were a prime example. Conductors might allow a black person to board a car as long as no white riders objected. Conductors could also—and often did—make black people wait for a car bearing the sign "Colored People Allowed in the Car."

On July 16, 1854, Elizabeth Jennings and her friend Sarah Adams were running late to church. They waved down a Third Avenue streetcar—one without a "colored people" sign.

From the start there was trouble. As the women tried to board, the conductor told them they should wait for another streetcar that had "their people" on it. Jennings refused to leave.

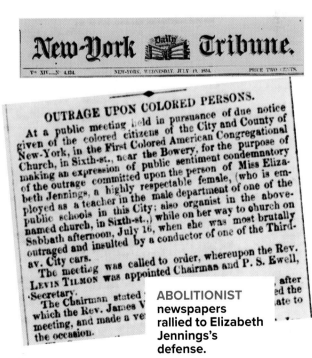

ABOLITIONIST newspapers rallied to Elizabeth Jennings's defense.

After a tense standoff, the conductor said he would let them on if no one complained.

This offended Jennings, as she would later relate: "[I] told him I was a respectable person, born and raised in New York . . . and that he was a good-for-nothing fellow for insulting decent persons while on their way to church."

Thrown into the Street

That did it. The conductor moved to push the women into the street. Adams was ejected, but Jennings put up a fierce struggle. She held on to a window frame and then the conductor's coat before he called to the driver for help. The two men nearly succeeded in pushing Jennings off the streetcar. When the driver went back to his horses, Jennings broke free from the conductor and entered the car.

RARE VIEW:
The only known photograph of Elizabeth Jennings

The car continued on until the driver hailed a policeman. Without listening to her, Jennings later wrote, the officer "thrust me out, and then pushed me."

At home, Jennings's father insisted that she write down what had happened. He then showed her account to the leaders of the black community, who called a meeting at a local church to decide on a plan of action.

Word spread quickly. The *New-York Daily Tribune*, an abolitionist newspaper, printed her story under the headline, "Outrage Upon Colored Persons."

A Future President Takes the Case

Jennings and her father decided to sue the Third Avenue Railroad Company. They hired an attorney named Chester Alan Arthur to take the case. Just 25 years old and fresh out of law school, Arthur later went on to become the 21st U.S. president, in 1881.

On February 22, 1855, Jennings's case was heard before a packed courtroom. Judge William Rockwell instructed the all-white male jury that the streetcar company should be in the business of serving "all respectable persons." The judge said, "Colored persons, if sober, well-behaved, and free from disease [have] the same rights as others."

After a day of testimony, the jury decided in Jennings's favor. She was awarded $225 in damages ($6,672 in 2020 dollars).

As a result of the Jennings case, the Third Avenue Railroad Company desegregated all of its cars. Most of the city's dozen or so other streetcar lines followed suit. But some streetcar companies refused to change. More importantly, segregation itself was still legal.

Determined to integrate all the streetcars, Thomas Jennings and other black leaders organized the Legal Rights Association (LRA). In churches, civic meetings, and newspapers, they called for black people to keep riding the remaining segregated streetcars, then sue if they were turned away. The LRA would cover their legal bills.

To Kyle Volk, a historian at the University of Montana, this **grassroots** crusade sounds very much like the fight for equality that changed Montgomery, Alabama—and the nation—a century later. "It's one of the earliest seeds of the civil rights movement," he says.

In 1864—10 years after Jennings's stand—New York's last segregated streetcar line opened all of its cars to black people. Segregation in public transportation in New York was formally outlawed by the state legislature in 1873.

A Tale Nearly Lost to History

Jennings remained dedicated to improving life for black people. In 1895, she founded the city's first kindergarten for black children.

But for the most part, history passed Elizabeth Jennings by. When she died in 1901, it was barely noted outside the black press.

Why? For starters, her story was almost immediately overshadowed by the Civil War (1861–65). Says Hearth: "Slavery was a much more urgent issue than the rights of free blacks in the North."

Jennings's struggle may not be famous, but her fight shows how far back the crusade for civil rights stretches—and that it was as important in the North as it was in the South.

"Her story," says Hearth, "helps Americans understand the full course of our history." ∎

ROSA PARKS is fingerprinted after she started the Montgomery, Alabama, bus boycott in 1955.

Luther Standing Bear's
Powerful Voice

In the late 1800s, thousands of Native American children, including Luther Standing Bear, were sent to boarding schools to "learn the ways of the white man." Luther became a powerful voice for his people.

Choose your new name," said the teacher. The 11-year-old boy looked at the marks on the blackboard. Having grown up speaking the language of his Lakota Sioux (pronounced SOO) people, he couldn't understand them. Now he had to pick one.

Of course he already had a name: Ota Kte (OH-tuh kuh-TAY). His father, the Lakota leader Standing Bear, had given it to him when he was born in 1868. Standing Bear had taught him how to ride a horse and hunt buffalo.

But Ota Kte was no longer with his people on the Pine Ridge **reservation** in what would later become South Dakota. Instead, he was 1,500 miles away in Carlisle, Pennsylvania. There, he was in the first class of students at the United States Indian Industrial School. The school was designed to teach him the ways of the white man—and erase his Native American identity.

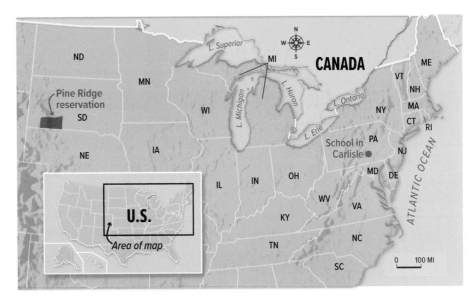

A LONG WAY FROM HOME: Luther's school was 1,500 miles from his reservation.

The boy recognized the challenge he faced: adapting to the world of the white people whose weapons and diseases had devastated his people. The name he chose was Luther. From that day on, Luther Standing Bear would live partly in the white man's world. But he would always carry his former life in his heart—and never stop fighting for his people.

Centuries of Struggle

By the time of Luther's renaming in 1879, America's Native people had been struggling against the control of white colonists for centuries. When Europeans began arriving in North America in the late 1400s, they claimed vast areas for themselves and their countries. But millions of people were already living there.

As white settlers moved west, Native Americans tried to hold on to their lands. Many died fighting the U.S. Army; millions of others were wiped out by diseases brought by the newcomers, such as smallpox and flu. By 1880, only 300,000 Native Americans remained in the U.S. Most had been forced off their lands and were living on reservations. The new lands were often hard to farm. Hunters could no longer roam. Many tribes faced hunger and despair.

America's leaders struggled with what to do about the country's Native inhabitants. Many believed Native people were too "savage" to have a role in society. Luther Standing Bear would become part of an attempt to address this: boarding schools.

The idea came from a U.S. Army officer named Richard Henry Pratt. Like most white

BEFORE & AFTER: Students were photographed soon after they arrived, and again later. Pictures like these impressed U.S. officials, who hoped the school would help "civilize" Native Americans.

Americans at the time, Pratt believed in the superiority of white culture. Yet he thought that if young Native people could be taught white values, they could succeed. Pratt said that the U.S. government should invest in boarding schools for Native children. There, the young people's heritage—their language and culture—would be stripped away. The schools would transform them into Pratt's idea of "true Americans." He convinced the government to let him test his idea. In 1879, Pratt founded a school at a former military barracks in Carlisle, Pennsylvania.

Keeping Connected to His People

In 1879, Ota Kte arrived at the school with dozens of other Lakota children. Luther received a military-style uniform and tight boots to wear; his deerskin leggings and moccasins were taken away, and he was forced to cut off his hair. Among Lakota men, long hair was a source of pride. As the barber got to work, "tears came into my eyes," Luther later wrote.

At the Carlisle school, students were forced to learn English and recite Christian prayers. But Luther stayed. He knew the old ways were gone. His people were now confined to a reservation. He couldn't become a warrior or hunt buffalo. But he could live up to his people's code in another way: by embracing his education.

Over time, Luther began to absorb white people's ways. He mastered English, went to Sunday school, and learned to play an instrument called the cornet. As a representative of his school, he worked at a department store in Philadelphia, where he excelled.

Still, Luther never lost his connection to his fellow Lakota. In 1884, after four years at the school, he realized something: "This was not the life I desired." He later wrote, "I told Captain Pratt I wanted to go home to my people." Pratt agreed to let his prized pupil leave.

An American Tragedy

The school in Carlisle was only the first of its kind. By 1910, about 60,000 Native American students were attending more than 150 such schools, most of them in the West. Many Native parents sent their children because they thought the schools would give them the tools to survive in a changing world. But many more kids were forced to go.

Students who graduated often struggled afterward. It was difficult to find jobs in the white world. Those who returned to their reservations often felt like strangers among their own people. Some had been away so long that they had forgotten their native languages.

In 1928, a government study exposed the terrible conditions in the schools. Influenced by the testimony of former students and the work of other Native American activists, officials gradually accepted that it was better for Native children to be educated in their own communities. The last Native boarding school finally closed in 1973.*

Fighting for His People

As for Luther, he returned to his people when he was 16. "I was caught between two worlds," he wrote. He later married and had children, became the principal of his reservation's school, and became a Lakota leader like his father. Yet in 1912, he moved away with his family, never to return.

He became a leading voice for Native American rights. He fought for bilingual education on reservations, Native history classes in U.S. schools, and preservation of the Lakota culture.

Until his death in 1939, Luther Standing Bear put his education from the Carlisle school to good use. But he never forgot the early lessons from his father about bravery, honor, and service to his people. And wherever he went, he was always a Lakota at heart. ■

LUTHER STANDING BEAR became a leader of the Ogala Lakota.

* Canada, Australia, and New Zealand had similar schools for their indigenous peoples.

The Quest for Women's Equality

PROMOTING women's suffrage in New York in 1914

Hillary Clinton didn't end up in the White House in 2016, but the election showed how far women have come since gaining the right to vote in 1920.

"**T**hanks to you, we've reached a milestone," **Hillary Clinton told supporters in** June 2016 after she clinched the Democratic nomination for president. Then she put the achievement in perspective: "Tonight's victory is not about one person. It belongs to generations of women and men who struggled and sacrificed and made this moment possible."

Indeed, Clinton's success in winning the top spot on the Democratic ticket is just the latest step in a long quest for women's equality in the U.S.

As early as the American Revolution (1775–83), women's roles in the U.S. were already being debated. In 1776, Abigail Adams wrote a letter to her husband and future president, John Adams, at the Continental Congress in Philadelphia. Abigail urged her husband to "remember the ladies" in any "new code of laws" that Congress devised. "[Women] will not hold ourselves bound by any laws in which we have no voice," she wrote.

Yet women had no voice in the government that came about after the Revolution. The Constitution, written in 1787, left many matters up to state governments. The states gave few rights to women, and only one, New Jersey, allowed women to vote (until 1807).

It was in 1848 that women's rights really took off, with the Women's Rights Convention in Seneca Falls, New York. Its Declaration of Sentiments and Resolutions, modeled on the Declaration of Independence, laid out objections to the treatment of women in education, work, and property ownership—and called for women's suffrage, the right to vote.

The women's suffrage movement was led by activists such as Lucretia Mott, Elizabeth Cady Stanton, Ida B. Wells, and Susan B. Anthony. Anthony's decades of crusading included casting a ballot in the presidential election of 1872, which led to her arrest and trial.

Tennessee and the 19th Amendment

In 1890, when Wyoming became a state, it was the first state to permanently allow women to vote. By 1914, women could vote in 11 of the 48 states.

At that time, there were few women in the workplace. Then, in 1917, the United States entered World War I (1914–18). As men went off to fight, women took over jobs on railroads and in factories.

In 1917, groups including the National Woman's Party **picketed** the White House, and President Woodrow Wilson came to endorse suffrage, which he called "vitally essential" to the war effort. In 1919, Congress passed the 19th Amendment to the Constitution, guaranteeing women the right to vote. It reads: "The right of citizens of the United States to vote shall not be denied or abridged by the United States or by any State on account of sex." As with all constitutional amendments, three-fourths of the 48 states had to ratify it.

SUFFRAGIST
Alice Paul works on a "19th Amendment Victory Flag" in the 1910s. After being arrested for protesting outside the White House, Paul went on a hunger strike in prison to protest the horrible conditions.

Most states in the Midwest, the East, and the West ratified the amendment. But some Southern states rejected it. By August 1920, 35 states had approved it—one fewer than the 36 required. In Tennessee lawmakers were deadlocked. Many amendment supporters thought it was a lost cause. But then state representative Harry Burn, a 24-year-old Republican who opposed the amendment, received a letter from his mother.

"Hurrah, and vote for suffrage!" she wrote, urging her son to "be a good boy." Burn listened to his mother. With that, women at last had a constitutional right to vote.

"Unfinished Business"

The 19th Amendment was a huge victory for women's rights. "Before the amendment, women were secondary," says Ruth B. Mandel, a political scientist at Rutgers University in New Jersey. "But passage of the suffrage amendment—that began to change everything."

In the decades that followed, women saw their roles expand in many areas. Today, women make up more than half of college undergraduates in the U.S. and about half of the workforce. Women have long served in America's wars. The Department of Defense recently announced that it was removing all remaining restrictions on women in combat positions.

Suffragists like Susan B. Anthony might be surprised to know how their fight for

Milestones in **Women's Rights**

1848
Elizabeth Cady Stanton is among the organizers of the Women's Rights Convention in Seneca Falls, New York, which calls for women's suffrage.

1916
Jeannette Rankin of Montana is the first woman elected to the U.S. House of Representatives. In 1932, Hattie Caraway of Arkansas becomes the first woman elected to the Senate.

1920
The 19th Amendment to the U.S. Constitution, guaranteeing the vote to women, is ratified.

1941–45
Millions of women take jobs vacated by men fighting in World War II. The subject of this popular poster, Rosie the Riveter, becomes an icon.

The 19th Amendment "began to change everything."

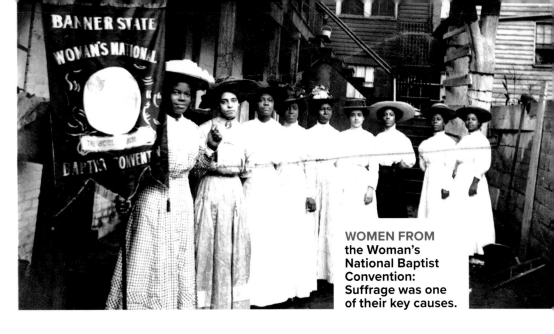

WOMEN FROM the Woman's National Baptist Convention: Suffrage was one of their key causes.

the vote has paid off. In the 2018 midterm elections, some 65 million women said they voted, compared with 57 million men. In 2020, of the nation's 100 U.S. senators, 25 were women—the highest proportion in history—and of the 435 voting members in the House of Representatives, 101 were female. On the Supreme Court, women accounted for three of the nine justices.

In a 2013 speech, Clinton spoke about the great strides in women's equality. "Let's learn from the wisdom of every mother and father who teaches their daughter that there is no limit on how big she can dream and how much she can achieve," Clinton said. "This truly is the unfinished business of the 21st century." ■

1968
Shirley Chisholm (Democrat of New York) is elected the first black Congresswoman.

1981
Sandra Day O'Connor becomes the first woman appointed to the Supreme Court.

2007
Congresswoman Nancy Pelosi (Democrat of California) is elected Speaker of the House.

2016
Hillary Clinton becomes the first female presidential nominee of a major party (Democratic).

2020
More women candidates than ever before run for president, and a record number sit in the House and Senate; the ERA (Equal Rights Amendment) is revived. (See p. 32.)

A Bold Act of Solidarity

When the U.S. government forced tens of thousands of Japanese Americans into prison camps during World War II, 17-year-old Ralph Lazo volunteered to go with them.

When Ralph Lazo, a high school student in Los Angeles, saw his Japanese American friends being forced from their homes and into **internment** camps during World War II, he did something unexpected: He went with them.

The U.S. government had set up the camps as a result of President Franklin D. Roosevelt's executive order to imprison Japanese Americans following Japan's surprise attack on Pearl Harbor in Hawaii in 1941. From 1942 to 1946, more than 115,000 people of Japanese ancestry in the western U.S.—two-thirds of them U.S. citizens and the rest legal immigrants—would be held in 10 camps located in barren areas of the country.

In the spring of 1942, after seeing his classmates get sent away, 17-year-old Ralph boarded a train and headed to the Manzanar Relocation Center, an internment camp in eastern California. Ralph didn't have to be there. A Mexican American, he was the only known person to pretend to be Japanese so he could be willingly incarcerated.

What compelled Ralph to give up his freedom for two and a half years—sleeping in tar-paper-covered barracks, using open latrines and showers, on grounds surrounded by barbed-wire fencing and watched by guards in towers? He wanted to be with his friends.

"My Japanese American friends at high school were ordered to evacuate the West Coast," Ralph told the *Los Angeles Times* in 1944, "so I decided to go along with them."

Locked Up for Their Ethnicity

Today the imprisonment of Japanese Americans during World War II is remembered as one of our nation's gravest injustices. Loyal Americans were locked up not because of any crimes they had committed, but simply because of their ethnicity.

The nation turned on its Japanese American citizens after the bombing of Pearl Harbor on December 7, 1941, which thrust the U.S. into World War II against Japan and its allies, Germany and Italy. Just hours after the attack, FBI agents raided the homes of Japanese Americans and religious leaders, jailing anyone suspected of secretly working for the enemy.

Asian immigrants in the U.S. had long faced discrimination, dating back to the 19th century, when tens of thousands of Chinese immigrants worked in gold mines and built railroads. The Chinese Exclusion Act of 1882 barred immigrants from China for 60 years. In 1924, Congress barred all ethnic Japanese except those born in the U.S. from gaining citizenship.

Anti-Japanese sentiment peaked after Pearl Harbor. Many politicians, the press, and military officials spread rumors that people of Japanese ancestry might help Japan if it invaded the West Coast. (Not one person of Japanese ancestry was ever charged with spying or sabotage during the war.)

FDR's Executive Order

On February 19, 1942, President Roosevelt signed Executive Order 9066, which authorized the military to designate zones in which certain people couldn't live.

By May, all people of Japanese ancestry in California, and parts of Washington, Oregon, and Arizona, were forced to abandon their homes, businesses, and schools. They were sent to 10 watchtower-guarded camps run by the army. (See map.)

Unlike most Americans, Ralph Lazo wasn't swept up by the anti-Japanese sentiment. His family lived near the Little Tokyo area of Los Angeles, and at Belmont High School, he counted Japanese Americans among his closest friends.

"Who Can Say I Haven't Got Japanese Blood in Me?"

As many were distancing themselves from their Japanese neighbors and colleagues—or worse, attacking them verbally

A PAGE FROM Ralph Lazo's school yearbook

JAPANESE INTERNMENT CAMP

SOURCE: National Japanese American Historical Society

or physically—his identification with his friends grew deeper.

"Who can say I haven't got Japanese blood in me?" he said in 1944. "Who knows what kind of blood runs in my veins?"

He told his father he was "going to camp," implying that he was going to summer camp. His father didn't press him, and neither did government officials, whose system for entry into the camps relied largely on self-reporting.

About 10,000 people were imprisoned at Manzanar, where they lived in military-style barracks in punishing summer desert heat. They slept on mattresses made of hay, ate meals of canned hot dogs, and were forced to work on the camp's farm or in its factories, making clothes and mattresses for little pay. Despite their grim surroundings, they recreated the rhythms of normal life by running schools, newspapers, and sports teams.

Many at Manzanar were aware of Ralph's ethnicity. One of his classmates at the camp, Rosie Kakuuchi, says that Ralph spent time amusing the orphaned children at Manzanar with games and jokes. "We accepted him and loved him," Kakuuchi, now in her 90s, says. "He was just one of us."

It wasn't until August 1944, when Ralph was drafted into the army, that the government discovered his secret. He didn't face any repercussions. In fact, the government issued a news release disclosing his unusual story. Ralph left the camp to serve in the Pacific until 1946, receiving a Bronze Star for bravery among other honors.

In 1944, the Supreme Court ruled that the government may not detain "loyal" citizens. In 1945, the War Department announced that internees were free to leave, and Japanese Americans began the difficult process of rebuilding their lives.

"We Can Take a Clear Stand for Justice"

After the war, Ralph maintained ties to the Japanese community. He attended Manzanar reunions and supported efforts to secure reparations for Japanese Americans.

In the 1950s and 1960s the civil rights movement inspired some younger Japanese Americans to speak out about the injustices their families had faced. They urged the government to issue an apology and pay reparations. In 1988, calling the internments "a grave wrong," President Ronald Reagan signed the Civil Liberties Act, which provided a $20,000 payment for each surviving internee. More than 80,000 people received a payment.

A letter sent out with the checks read: "A monetary sum and words alone cannot restore lost years. . . . But we can take a clear stand for justice." ■

LABOR ACTIVIST Cesar Chavez (center) talks with grape pickers about joining a farmworkers' union.

Justice for Farmworkers

Cesar Chavez's protests won better conditions for U.S. farmworkers—and gave them new hope.

Farmworkers perform backbreaking labor to provide millions of people with food. Despite the important work these men and women perform, their employers have not always treated them fairly.

Cesar Chavez, like many farmworkers in the United States, came from a family of Mexican immigrants. He started picking crops alongside his family in the fields of California in the 1940s, when he was still a child. At the time, a California farmworker might make less than 50 cents an hour. The Chavez family traveled all around the state to pick crops at different farms at different times of year. Even though the whole family worked hard, they barely made enough money to get by. Their story was not unique. Countless other migrant workers shared the same difficulties.

In the 1950s, after serving a short time in the U.S. Navy, Chavez returned home to California and started working with labor leaders to help the state's farmworkers. He met with people across the region, talked with them about workers' rights, and encouraged them to vote in elections. He also helped organize strikes to pressure farm owners into paying fairer wages.

In 1962, Chavez began organizing a union of farmworkers, working closely with fellow activist Dolores Huerta. Calling the union the National Farm Workers Association (NFWA), Chavez began traveling throughout California in search of supporters. Three years later, he led the union's first strike and secured a pay increase for workers on a rose farm. The NFWA had won its first victory, but it was only the beginning.

Inspired by the tactics of activists such as Mahatma Gandhi in India and civil rights leader Martin Luther King Jr., Chavez believed that peaceful protests were the most effective way to make a difference. Throughout the 1960s, he organized a series of strikes, marches, boycotts, and even hunger strikes to spread awareness of the plight of farmworkers and to pressure farm owners to negotiate.

In 1966, the NFWA merged with another farmworkers' union to form the United Farm Workers (UFW), which remains active today. Under Chavez's leadership, the union won health care, better pay, and improved working conditions for tens of thousands of workers. Today, Chavez remains an important symbol of organized labor and civil rights for immigrants. ■

CHAVEZ LEADS strikers and supporters during a strike in Delano, California.

SIT-IN LEADERS (from left) Joseph McNeil and Franklin McCain with friends who joined them on the second day of protests at the Woolworth's lunch counter in Greensboro

Sitting Down to Take a Stand

In 1960, four black students asked to be served at an all-white lunch counter in North Carolina and jump-started the civil rights movement.

Just after 4 p.m. on February 1, 1960, four black college students, dressed in their Sunday best, walked into the F. W. Woolworth department store in downtown Greensboro, North Carolina. After buying some school supplies and other items, they sat down at the all-white lunch counter and tried to order a cup of coffee.

"We don't serve Negroes* here," a waitress said.

"We are going to sit here until we are served," one of the students, Jibreel Khazan,** replied.

> **"We are going to sit here until we are served."**

*Negroes, once used to describe African Americans, is now considered out-of-date and offensive.
**Jibreel Khazan was born Ezell Blair Jr. He changed his name in 1968.

Khazan and his classmates—Joseph McNeil, Franklin McCain, and David Richmond—never did get served that day. But the four freshmen from North Carolina A&T State, a historically black university in Greensboro, remained seated. That simple act of defiance more than 60 years ago would change history, inspiring a massive movement of sit-ins and other protests against segregation in scores of cities throughout the South. From that moment forward, those students would forever be known as the Greensboro Four.

"The spontaneous courage of those four young men, who simply decided the night before, 'let's do something,' triggered a whole movement of sit-ins around the South, and supporting demonstrations in other places," says Frye Gaillard, a historian who has written several books about the South. "I would argue that it jump-started the civil rights movement."

The Jim Crow South

Six years before the Greensboro sit-ins, the Supreme Court had ruled in *Brown v. Board of Education* that segregated public schools were unconstitutional, overturning the "separate but equal" principle that had been established by the court in 1896 in *Plessy v. Ferguson*. In

WAITING ROOMS like this one in North Carolina and other public facilities across the South were segregated during the Jim Crow era.

"It's time for someone to wake up and change the situation."

addition, the 1955–56 bus boycott in Montgomery, Alabama, led by Rosa Parks and Martin Luther King Jr., prompted a Supreme Court decision barring segregation on public buses.

But by the end of the 1950s, most public facilities in the South were still segregated—and rarely equal. State and local laws that enforced segregation in the South—known as Jim Crow laws—remained on the books. "Whites Only" signs were plastered above lunch counters, water fountains, waiting rooms, and bathrooms, and in restaurants and hotels across the region.

Though a few sit-ins had been staged in other southern cities, they were mostly isolated events that failed to capture the attention of the nation. The growing civil rights movement seemed to be moving slowly, as leaders of the National Association for the Advancement of Colored People (NAACP) argued that the best way to challenge segregation was in the courts—a process that took years.

In the fall of 1959, the four freshmen at North Carolina A&T began to grow impatient with the slow pace of progress. They met often in their dorm rooms, talking about racial injustice, King's philosophy of nonviolence, and what they could do to make a difference. Their discussions took on more urgency after Christmas break that year, when McNeil was refused service at a rest stop in Richmond, Virginia, while traveling back to school from his family's home in New York City. The next time the four best friends met in their dorm, they began to devise a plan to turn their late-night talks into action.

"Adults have been complacent and fearful," Khazan later recalled saying. "It's time for someone to wake up and change the situation."

"And we decided to start here," he explained.

The Greensboro Four

"Here" was the Woolworth's in Greensboro, North Carolina, part of one of the world's largest retail chains. It was a typical "five and dime" that sold all kinds of merchandise for less than a dollar, and its lunch counter served about 2,000 meals a day.

When it came to serving black people at the lunch counter, the policy of the F. W. Woolworth Company, based in New York, was to "abide by local custom." In the North, blacks sat alongside whites at Woolworth's, but not in the South.

On February 1, 1960, the four young men made purchases at other sales counters in

POURING ketchup, mustard, and drinks on protesters sitting in at a Woolworth's in Jackson, Mississippi, 1963

the Greensboro store to prove that they had been served and their money accepted. Then they quietly sat down at the lunch counter, expecting the worst.

"We tried to imagine all the possibilities," McCain said decades later. "One was I was going to go to jail for a long time and never come back to school. Or the other: I was going to be trying to pick my brains up off the floor and maybe come back to my campus in a casket. But it meant just that much to me."

After McCain and his friends ignored the waitresses' orders to leave, the manager of the lunch counter was summoned. He told the four young men to stop causing trouble. But they quietly remained seated. Several white customers got up and left the store, and a police officer arrived. Standing over the students, he pounded his nightstick into the palm of his hand. Sweat began to build on the students' foreheads. Still, they refused to move.

"A Movement for All People"

The Greensboro Four made it until the store closed without being arrested—a small victory, but enough to encourage them to come back the next day and the next. On the third day, they were joined by about 80 other protesters, who took turns sitting at the counter and praying and picketing outside the store. Before long, there were more than 1,000 of them, including fellow classmates from A&T; students from Bennett, a historically black women's college in Greensboro; and from the segregated black high school, Dudley High. Reporters from all over the country for newspapers, radio, and a relatively new medium, television, came to cover the sit-in.

But opposition also arrived: hordes of white counterprotesters who tried to take Woolworth's stools to prevent the black students from sitting there.

The white protesters viciously heckled the black demonstrators, and a bomb threat was called into the store one afternoon, forcing it to close early. But footage of black students opening their books at the counter and studying peacefully in the face of violent threats had begun to make national news.

"A lunch counter sit-in is more photographically powerful than an empty bus," says David Garrow, author of a Pulitzer Prize–winning biography of King, "and abusive behavior by white onlookers captures the inherent nastiness of racism in clear and memorable fashion."

The protests spread rapidly. By the end of February, sit-ins were taking place in at least 30 communities in eight southern states.

"It was a movement for all people," Khazan recalled.

A group of students capitalized on the momentum of the sit-ins to form the Student Nonviolent Coordinating Committee (SNCC). The student-led organization, whose leaders included John Lewis (who became a long-time congressman from Georgia), drew young volunteers of all races to participate in civil rights protests and voter registration drives.

Nonviolent Civil Disobedience

Back in Greensboro, the demonstrations at the Woolworth's continued for nearly six months and soon included other stores. Finally, in July 1960, after the Woolworth's had lost $1.7 million (in today's dollars), history was made. The store manager invited three black employees to sit and be served. The lunch counter was officially desegregated.

The success in Greensboro was just the start. By the end of the year, it was estimated that as many as 70,000 protesters had participated in sit-ins and picketing across the South that had resulted in some 3,000 arrests.

Some demonstrators faced abuse and were badly injured. Many had undergone training in nonviolent civil disobedience, practicing how to remain peaceful and not respond to physical and verbal attacks. Over the next four years, students took part in similar protests not just at lunch counters, but at public pools, libraries, movie theaters, and other segregated facilities.

The young protesters were often chastised for being too "radical." A 1961 Gallup poll showed that a majority of the American public believed that the sit-ins would harm the civil rights movement. Even many older civil rights leaders were wary, urging the students to slow things down.

Student Energy

Nevertheless, they persisted. Their peaceful protests and others like them helped galvanize support in Congress and in the country for the Civil Rights Act of 1964, which barred segregation in all public places and businesses. It might not have passed until later, historians say, if not for the actions of young people who refused to wait for things to change.

A PROTESTER holds a Black Lives Matter sign at a rally in New York City.

"So much of the energy of the southern movement was student energy," says Garrow, "the willingness of young people who had not yet fully begun their adult lives to step into full-time civil rights work."

Beyond playing a vital role in the civil rights movement, SNCC also propelled many young people into the anti-Vietnam War movement. Students across the country held rallies on college campuses and marched on Capitol Hill in the 1960s and 1970s to protest the war.

Today, there's a reinvigorated activism among students. Many have joined movements such as Black Lives Matter to protest police brutality against black people. They've participated in demonstrations such as the Climate March to demand action on global warming, and March for Our Lives to call for an end to gun violence. Many historians say the Greensboro sit-ins continue to serve as a model for these present-day movements.

In 2010, the Woolworth's in Greensboro was transformed into the International Civil Rights Center & Museum. Most of the lunch counter is still there.

At the museum's opening ceremony, Franklin McCain offered this advice to young people: "Don't ever ask permission to start a revolution." ■

1960: Ruby Bridges

Ruby Bridges was only six years old when she made history by becoming the first black student to attend a previously all-white school in New Orleans, Louisiana.

In 1954, the Supreme Court ruled in *Brown v. Board of Education of Topeka* that segregation in public schools was unconstitutional. But many schools did everything they could to keep black students out.

In 1960, New Orleans's William Frantz Elementary School held a test that black students had to pass before they would be allowed to attend. Ruby Bridges was one of six students to pass, and the only one who ultimately decided to enroll in the school.

On November 14, 1960, Ruby walked up the stairs of the school to begin her first day. Though she had to pass by screaming, angry protesters every morning, Ruby bravely kept her head held high and didn't miss a single day of school that year. ■

1963: The Birmingham Children's Crusade

In 1963, civil rights activists had been trying to pressure Birmingham, Alabama, into ending segregation, but their sit-ins and protests had no effect.

The children of Birmingham were also eager for change. When an activist named James Bevel asked for young volunteers, hundreds responded.

On May 2, 1963, more than 1,000 black kids—some as young as seven—calmly marched toward the city's business district. The police arrested and jailed hundreds of them. The next day, even more kids marched, and they were slammed by water from fire hoses and attacked by police dogs. Day after day, thousands more marched and were jailed.

The images shocked the nation. President John F. Kennedy (1961–63) tried to resolve the crisis. After eight days, the city agreed to stop enforcing segregation laws and released the kids from jail. ■

MARTIN LUTHER KING JR. (center) marches in Selma, Alabama, in 1965 for black voting rights; future member of Congress John Lewis of Georgia is at right.

A Half-Century After MLK: Where Are We Now?

The 1968 assassination of Martin Luther King Jr. stunned the nation, but his work continues to inspire the pursuit of racial equality in America.

On August 28, 1963, more than 250,000 people gathered on the National Mall in Washington, D.C., to hear one of the most powerful speeches in history. A young Baptist minister named Martin Luther King Jr. addressed the crowd at the March on Washington, a protest rally he helped organize.

"I have a dream," King said, "that one day this nation will rise up [and] live out the true meaning of its creed: We hold these truths to be self-evident, that all men are created equal."

His words were a call for racial equality and racial justice for African Americans. The march—an example of the nonviolent protest King advocated—helped secure passage of the Civil Rights Act of 1964. That landmark legislation outlawed racial segregation in schools and the workplace and at public facilities. The act was one of many civil rights milestones in which King played a key role. (See p. 172.)

Just a few years later, his life was cut short. In 1968, he was assassinated in

Memphis, Tennessee, at the age of 39. Millions around the nation and the world mourned King. "The heart of America grieves today," said President Lyndon B. Johnson (1963–69). "A leader of his people—a teacher of all people—has fallen."

More than 50 years after King's death, great strides have been made toward achieving civil rights for all Americans. But his dream of full equality has yet to be realized, says Hasan Jeffries, a professor of African American history at Ohio State University. "The very same issues that people are wrestling with now—police violence and unarmed African Americans being killed, people taking to the streets for affordable housing—are the same issues King was wrestling with then."

From Minister to Activist

A native of Atlanta, Georgia, King never intended to be the face of the civil rights movement. He started out as a minister in Montgomery, Alabama, in 1954. The Civil War had been over for nearly a century, yet, throughout the South, Jim Crow laws, racist customs, and segregation were a way of life.

Though he had little experience in activism, King was a brilliant public speaker. In 1955, community leaders recruited him to be the spokesman for the Montgomery bus boycott. The boycott lasted for more than a year and resulted in the Supreme Court declaring racial segregation on public buses unconstitutional.

King also played a pivotal role in securing voting rights for African Americans. In 1965, he helped organize the march from Selma, Alabama, to the state capital of Montgomery. This protest led to President Johnson signing the Voting Rights Act of 1965. That law made literacy tests and other obstacles to black voter registration illegal.

MARTIN LUTHER KING meets with President Lyndon B. Johnson at the White House in 1966.

As one of the most recognizable faces of the civil rights era, King was a target of those who opposed the movement. He was beaten and jailed, and his home was bombed. He received frequent death threats. Yet even in the face of such violence, King

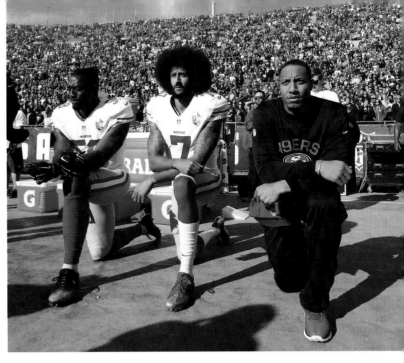

remained peaceful, says biographer David Garrow: "King was first and foremost a preacher. He would always insist upon distinguishing between the evil deed and the evil doer. He was incapable of hating."

King continued to speak out, even taking a stand in 1967 against U.S. involvement in the Vietnam War (1954–75). By 1968, King had begun campaigning for housing rights for minorities and was preparing a rally in Washington to raise awareness of poverty. "What good is having the right to sit at a lunch counter," he asked, "if you can't afford to buy a hamburger?"

KING ADVOCATED the kind of nonviolent protest that Colin Kaepernick (center) exercised by kneeling during the national anthem in 2016.

King's assassination in April 1968 cut all that short. But within days of his death, Congress passed the Fair Housing Act, which banned discrimination in housing and was seen as a tribute to King.

If King Had Lived . . .

King's work helped pave the way for many important African American firsts, including the election of the first black president, Barack Obama, in 2008.

Still, America continues to struggle with some of the same problems. Many black people still lack the same economic or educational opportunities as white people. And police killings of unarmed African Americans have ignited massive protests.

Many people believe that if King were alive today, he would support groups protesting for change, including football players who kneel during the national anthem to draw attention to police brutality; fast-food workers demanding a raise; and the Black Lives Matter movement.

King would also be reminding us, historians say, that all the positive changes that have happened in this country are due to people's willingness to fight for them.

"You don't need a lot of people to make an impact," Jeffries says. "[When] a small fraction of people organize and come together and speak with one voice, they can make a big difference." ■

TIMELINE: Highlights of the Civil Rights Movement

1954 – *Brown v. Board of Education*

The U.S. Supreme Court rules that segregated public schools are unconstitutional.

1955 – Montgomery Bus Boycott

Rosa Parks is arrested in Montgomery, Alabama, for refusing to give up her bus seat to a white passenger, sparking a boycott of city buses.

1957 – The Little Rock Nine

Nine black students are blocked from entering all-white Central High School in Little Rock, Arkansas. Eventually, federal troops escort the students inside.

1960 – Woolworth's Sit-In, North Carolina

Four black college students stage a sit-in at a whites-only lunch counter in Greensboro. Six months later, the lunch counter agrees to serve black people.

1963 – "I Have a Dream"

More than 250,000 people participate in the March on Washington. Martin Luther King Jr. delivers his famous speech on the steps of the Lincoln Memorial.

1964 – Civil Rights Act

President Lyndon B. Johnson signs the Civil Rights Act of 1964, which outlaws segregation in education, employment, and public facilities.

1965 – Voting Rights Act

President Johnson signs the Voting Rights Act of 1965, which makes literacy tests and other obstacles to black voter registration illegal.

Remembering Matthew Shepard

The brutal killing of a gay Wyoming college student in 1998 raised awareness about violence against the LGBTQ community and led to an expansion of hate-crime laws.

Matthew Shepard wanted to make a difference in the world. As a student at Natrona County High School in Casper, Wyoming, he was elected a peer counselor and dreamed of working for the U.S. State Department. "He thought it would be great to serve his country," says Dennis Shepard, Matthew's dad.

But Shepard never got to realize his dream. Just after midnight on October 7, 1998, when Shepard was a 21-year-old senior at the University of Wyoming, two men kidnapped him and drove him to a field outside Laramie, Wyoming. They brutally beat him, tied him to a fence, and left him to die in the freezing cold—all because he was gay.

"It was horrifying," says Dennis Shepard, "the brutality of it and the lack of morality."

In his death, Matthew Shepard became a symbol for the fight against bigotry and hate. The horrific murder made headlines across the nation and galvanized a movement that put a spotlight on violence against the LGBTQ (lesbian, gay, bisexual, transgender, queer/questioning) community and led to more hate-crime legislation.

Before Shepard's death, many people didn't realize how much violence against LGBTQ people took place. "I think that's why a lot of people were so stunned; they thought things were starting to change," says Jay Brown of the Human Rights Campaign. "And then they realized that being visibly gay could still be a matter of life and death."

When Shepard died on October 12, President Bill Clinton (1993–2001) gave a speech condemning his attackers. "Crimes of hate and crimes of violence cannot be tolerated in our country," he said. "In our shock and grief, one thing must remain clear: Hate and prejudice are not American values."

Two days later, thousands of people gathered in front of the Capitol in Washington, D.C., to mourn Shepard's death and demand change. Thousands more marched in New York City, and people all across the country held vigils. Many believed that they or someone they knew could easily be in Shepard's place.

SHEPARD WAS TIED to this fence outside Laramie, Wyoming.

"The Kid Next Door"

"Everybody saw something, regardless of their race or religion or skin color, in Matthew that they could see either in themselves or somebody in their family," Dennis Shepard says. "He was the kid next door."

But while mourners flocked to the vigils, so did anti-gay protesters. They held signs saying Shepard would "rot in hell" and screamed at Shepard's parents as they entered a church in Wyoming for a memorial service.

Police arrested two 21-year-olds, Aaron McKinney and Russell Henderson, and charged them with kidnapping and murdering Shepard. According to police reports, McKinney and Henderson approached Shepard at a bar in Laramie on October 6. Later that night, they lured him into their truck by pretending they were also gay.

They drove Shepard to a field, where they beat him on the head with a pistol, tied him to a wooden fence, and left him unconscious and bleeding. Shepard was so battered that a bicyclist who found him 18 hours later first mistook him for a scarecrow. McKinney and Henderson were convicted of murder and sentenced to two life terms in prison.

After Shepard's death, his parents and activists were determined not to let his story end there. For 10 years, they called on Congress to pass stricter legislation that would protect LGBTQ people against hate crimes. "We felt we owed it to Matt to try to make life better for his friends and peers," says Judy Shepard, Matthew's mom.

Gay marriage has been a constitutional right since 2015.

Combating Bigotry and Hate

In 2009, the Matthew Shepard and James Byrd Jr. Hate Crimes Prevention Act was signed into law by President Barack Obama (2009–17). Named for Shepard and Byrd—a black man murdered by three white supremacists in Texas the same year as Shepard—the act expanded the federal hate-crime law to include crimes motivated by bias against sexual orientation, gender identity, or disability.

Since Shepard's death, America overall has grown more accepting. In 2016, 63 percent of Americans said that homosexuality should be accepted by society, up from 51 percent in 2006, according to the Pew Research Center. In 2015, the Supreme Court ruled that gay marriage is a constitutional right. (See p. 89.) In 2020, there were 10 openly gay members of Congress.

However, two decades after Shepard's death, violence against the LGBTQ community hasn't gone away. According to the FBI, more than 1,200 hate crimes targeted people based on their sexual orientation or gender identity in 2017. (The actual number of hate crimes is probably higher, because many states don't collect or disclose this data.)

Judy Shepard has dedicated her life to speaking out against this type of bigotry and hate. Despite the prevalence of hate crimes, Judy Shepard still believes a better future for young LGBTQ people is possible.

"I want them to know there's hope," she says. "I want them to know the world is going to be a better place in the future, and to not ever give up." ∎

DENNIS AND JUDY Shepard at the White House with President Obama for the signing of the Matthew Shepard and James Byrd Jr. Hate Crimes Prevention Act

Matthew Shepard Was My Friend

Why Shepard's high school classmate continues to tell his story.

By Michele Josue

Shepard and Josue in 1995

In 1998, Matthew Shepard became an icon, a historical figure associated with unspeakable violence and hate. But to me, he was my friend Matt.

Matt and I attended a boarding high school in Switzerland. He was a junior and I was a freshman when we met. We both loved the theater and acted in school plays together. Matt was so full of life and curious about the world, and I learned a lot about what it means to be a good friend from him.

I was 19 when I learned of his death. My sister called me after seeing his face all over the news. It was the first time I saw how cruel the world could be. As I grew older, I felt a sense of urgency to share my friend's story so others could see the Matt I knew: a normal kid who was no different from any of us.

In 2010, I set out to make a documentary film about Matt, and began interviewing everyone from his parents to the bartender who last saw him and his murderers. Our film, *Matt Shepard Is a Friend of Mine*, was released five years later.

While we've come a long way in the two decades since my friend's murder, LGBTQ inequality and hate crimes are still very real today, and parts of Matt's story are unfortunately still a part of many young people's realities.

But by continuing to tell Matt's story, I want young people to learn that they have the power to create a more compassionate world—one in which we can prevent crimes like this from taking place.

While making the film, Father Roger Schmit, a priest in Laramie, Wyoming, told me something I carry with me to this day.

"I hope you never lose being angry" at violence and hate, Schmit said.

"Maybe his friends, their most important mission is to remind the world to be angry at that." ■

Should Bail Be Abolished?

The bail system is under fire from critics who say it's unfair to the poor and should be scrapped. But many in law enforcement say that's a dangerous idea.

Bail—money given to a court in exchange for an accused person's release from jail before trial—is meant to ensure that suspects who are let out of jail don't flee while their cases are being decided. The judge gives defendants who aren't considered dangerous or a flight risk the option to post bail which is paid to the court. People often have to borrow money to post bail. As long as the suspect makes all scheduled appearances, the money is returned when the case concludes.

Critics say the system is unfair to low-income people who sit in jail only because they can't come up with the money. Some states are reforming their systems or doing away with cash bail entirely, but many police officials and district attorneys say it creates a serious risk to public safety.

Turn the page to see how the two sides present their arguments in this debate. →

DEBATE

When Maranda ODonnell, a 22-year-old single mother, was arrested in May 2016 in Houston, Texas, for driving with an expired license, the judge set her bail at $2,500. ODonnell, who worked as a waitress, could not afford to pay, so she spent three days in jail, and missed time at work.

The same day ODonnell was pulled over, 37-year-old David Dorsey was arrested by Houston police and charged with the more serious crime of felony burglary. Two courtrooms over from ODonnell, Dorsey's bail was set at $30,000, which he quickly posted, leaving jail the following morning.

On any given day, there are 450,000 people in U.S. jails awaiting trial. Those who can afford to post bail are released, while poorer suspects can spend days, weeks, even months behind bars as their cases work their way through the courts.

"The bail system determines who is free and who is in a cage based solely on access to money," says Alec Karakatsanis, a civil rights attorney in Washington, D.C. "It's about who's rich and who's poor."

Until about 40 years ago, bail was used almost exclusively to ensure defendants came to court to face charges. But a crime wave in the 1970s led many lawmakers and judges to take a tougher approach, with laws passed to allow judges to set bail high to keep people in jail. The result was a sharp increase in the jail population. Even people facing charges for minor, nonviolent crimes could be held for weeks or months because they could not afford bail.

That victimizes the poor, and it is why a number of states are reforming their bail laws. California has eliminated bail entirely; in 2017, New Jersey eliminated bail for minor crimes like petty theft, simple assault and trespassing. According to the president of the New Jersey state senate, "We've reduced the number of people in jail without an increase in crime."

As for claims that bail reform puts dangerous people on the streets, Karakatsanis argues that the evidence doesn't support it. "The public safety argument is ridiculous," he says. "Most people that can't afford bail aren't violent criminals—they're simply poor." ■

Your bank account shouldn't determine if you're in jail.

DEBATE POINTS

★ Cash bail is unfair to the poor: Suspects go free if they can afford the bail, but sit in jail if they can't.
★ States that have reformed or abolished cash bail are no less safe than they were before.
★ Bail reform has helped decrease the number of people in jail across the U.S.

NO **The idea of bail has its roots in medieval England, where sheriffs used it to prevent criminal suspects from running off during the months-long wait for a judge to visit their villages.** In the U.S., the Framers recognized the value of bail, while including a protection against "excessive bail" in the Constitution's Eighth Amendment (known for its ban on "cruel and unusual punishments").

Many in law enforcement say that eliminating bail leads to a revolving door of arrest and release, and creates a serious risk to public safety.

"A cop can't protect the public when the guy he arrests is released before the police report is filled out," says James Stewart Jr. of the Fraternal Order of Police. "That only creates a bad guy who isn't worried about the police."

He points to the case of Kareem Dawson, who was arrested on domestic violence charges and released without bail twice in 2017 in New Jersey. In February 2018, Dawson murdered his girlfriend and then killed himself after a police chase.

"Because of bail reform, he was out on the street," says Stewart. "If a judge had set bail, he wouldn't have been able to pay and would have been in jail instead of out murdering this woman."

In New York City, both the mayor and the police commissioner attribute a sharp increase in crime at the beginning of 2020 to a new state law banning bail for most nonviolent crimes.

Part of the problem is that the definition in New York State of "nonviolent crimes" includes, according to the *New York Times*, types of stalking, assault, burglary, drug offenses, arson, and robbery.

The police commissioner says that suspects released from jail because of the new bail law have committed additional crimes. After a public outcry from people who believe that the reforms are spurring a dangerous rise in crime, the New York state legislature is considering a "reform" of "bail reform." Rolling back some of the changes that were made would restore judges' ability to help keep New York safe. ■

The bail system keeps many dangerous criminals off the streets.

DEBATE POINTS
- ★ Many police officers and district attorneys say eliminating bail puts dangerous people back on the streets where they can, and do, commit more crimes.
- ★ Broad definitions of "nonviolent crimes" increase the likelihood that dangerous suspects will quickly return to the street.
- ★ In New York and several states, changes to bail have led to increases in crime.

Progress, However Slow

As you've seen from all the stories in the civil rights unit, progress comes slowly, sometimes painfully, and sometimes violently. The two cartoonists here speak to the progress that has been made, but in a quiet, almost reverential way. There are no cheering crowds, just Americans playing their part in moving the nation forward, even if slowly, and with strength and resilience.

The top cartoon shows the Martin Luther King Jr. Memorial on the National Mall in Washington, D.C. It opened to the public in 2011. The bottom cartoon commemorates the record number of women—101 out of 435—in the House of Representatives after the 2018 midterm elections. They represent 34 states; 88 are Democrats and 13 are Republicans. ■

Analyze the Cartoons

1. The people in the top cartoon are using a common phrase as they "move" King's statue. What is the phrase and what does it mean in daily life?

2. What does the phrase mean in the context of the struggle for civil rights?

3. "A woman's place is in the House" echoes what once-common phrase expressing a traditional view of women's roles?

4. The cartoonist is playing on that phrase to show what?

Immigration: Who Gets to Be an American?

Benjamin Franklin worried about German immigrants taking over Pennsylvania. The 300-year debate over immigration continues today.

Going back to where she came from—

FRANCE

©Clay Bennett
Chattanooga Times Free Press Bennett

FIND MORE ONLINE: www.scholastic.com/howamericaworks

TIMELINE

Immigration in the U.S.

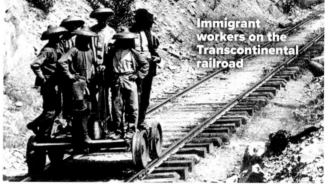

Immigrant workers on the Transcontinental railroad

Settlers welcoming new arrivals to Jamestown, Virginia

Gold Rush & Transcontinental Railroad

The California gold rush attracts Chinese immigrants who later help build the first transcontinental railroad. In 1882, Congress bars Chinese immigration.

PRE-1767

1849

1845

1892

Colonial Period

- There are hundreds of Native American cultures in what is today the United States when European settlers arrive.
- In the 250 years before independence, most settlers are from the British Isles; German immigrants settle mainly in Pennsylvania.
- Not all immigration was voluntary. Starting in 1619, Africans are brought to the colonies as slaves.

The Potato Famine

Widespread starvation in Ireland prompts massive emigration; 2 million Irish head to the U.S. in a decade.

Ellis Island

The main entry point into the U.S. opens in New York Harbor, near the Statue of Liberty; it closes in 1954.

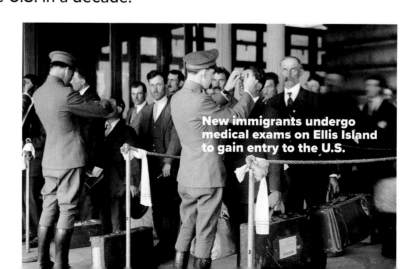

New immigrants undergo medical exams on Ellis Island to gain entry to the U.S.

Immigration soars in the late 19th century

Poverty & Persecution

Poverty and religious persecution spur an influx of Polish, Russian, Jewish, and Italian immigrants.

Quotas Abolished

The Immigration and Nationality Act of 1965 abolishes quotas. The U.S. sees an influx of Asians, Latinos, and others.

A protest for "Dreamers"

The Undocumented

The nation is sharply divided over immigration and what to do about the 11 million undocumented immigrants in the U.S.

1860s–1880s

1965

TODAY

1921

2001

Quotas by Nationality

Congress imposes immigration **quotas** that favor northern Europeans over southern and Eastern Europeans and everyone else.

9/11 Attacks

In response to the September 11 attacks, the USA PATRIOT Act tightens immigration with stricter border security.

Swedish immigrants in the Midwest

The World Trade Center in New York during the 9/11 attacks

THEN:
Immigrants arrive at Ellis Island in New York Harbor in the late 1800s.

What Makes Immigration So Controversial?

The debate over who is welcome in the United States stretches back to the nation's founding. Why are we still so divided?

While immigration is generating intense controversy today, the debate is nothing new. "Throughout American history, there has always been a tussle over immigration," says Alan Kraut, a history professor at American University in Washington, D.C.

"We have admitted millions of people because we needed their labor, their talents, their bodies, to settle our vast territories and work in our factories," he says. "At the same time, we've resisted their presence."

Who gets to be an American? That's the question at the heart of the immigration debate that consumed Washington, D.C., and the nation during Donald Trump's presidency. After he took office in 2017, his administration moved to dramatically reshape U.S. immigration policy.

Trump's policies resulted in many more arrests and deportations of undocumented immigrants, including raids on 7-Elevens and food-processing plants. The Trump administration tried to end a program protecting young people, known as Dreamers, who were brought to the U.S. illegally—and involuntarily—as children. By 2020, the number of refugees—many escaping war and religious persecution—admitted to the U.S. was the lowest in decades, and there were new restrictions on legal immigration. These changes in immigration policy led to many more people being held at the U.S.-Mexico border, with children often separated from their parents and sometimes kept in cages.

The United States, in many ways, is a nation of immigrants. But Americans are divided about what kind of immigration to allow and from where, and whether to permit people in the U.S. illegally to stay.

President Trump raised the temperature of the debate. His pledge to build a wall along the entire U.S.-Mexico border was cheered by his supporters but criticized by many others. The administration's travel ban on people from several majority-Muslim countries, announced as part of tighter security measures, prompted outrage and lawsuits.

Ben Franklin Worries About a "Colony of Aliens"

Conflicted feelings about immigration go back to the nation's founding. In 1776, most Americans were immigrants, or the descendants of immigrants, from the British Isles. The majority were white Anglo-Saxon Protestants who came for economic opportunity or to escape religious or political persecution.

But the population also included large numbers of Native Americans, people of Dutch or Spanish ancestry, and German immigrants, in addition to Africans, who were brought against their will as slaves beginning in 1619.

Americans have often been wary of welcoming foreigners. Even before the nation's founding, Benjamin Franklin worried that German

NOW:
A New York rally in support of "Dreamers" — young people who were brought here illegally, and involuntarily, as children.

immigrants were taking over Pennsylvania. In 1751, he referred to the German newcomers as "a colony of aliens [who] will never adopt our language or customs."

The 19th century brought a more diverse group of people, starting with Irish immigrants and later Italians. Both groups were largely poor farmers and Roman Catholic, not Protestant, like most Americans at that time. Immigration from Germany and Scandinavian countries like Denmark, Sweden, and Norway, also soared. Chinese immigrants began arriving in large numbers during the California gold rush (1849–55), followed later in the 19th century by Jews fleeing persecution in Russia and eastern Europe.

Before 1875, there were few restrictions on immigration. America's westward expansion, the Industrial Revolution, and the abolition of slavery created enormous demand

Where America's Immigrants Come from Today

Top countries of origin for all foreign-born people in the United States, as of 2018. Which continents account for the most immigrants?

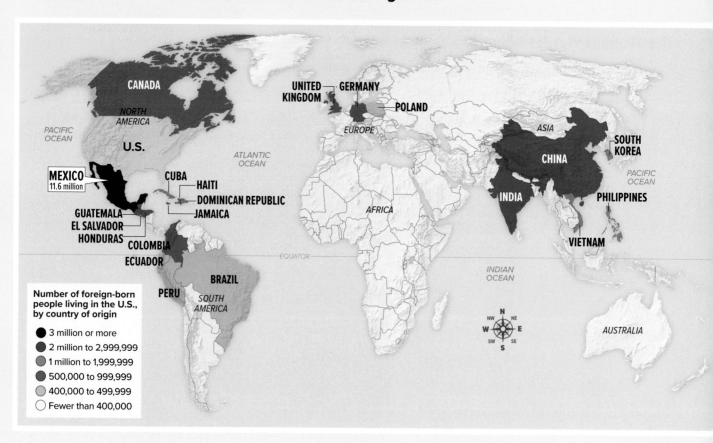

Number of foreign-born people living in the U.S., by country of origin

- ● 3 million or more
- ● 2 million to 2,999,999
- ● 1 million to 1,999,999
- ● 500,000 to 999,999
- ● 400,000 to 499,999
- ○ Fewer than 400,000

for labor on farms and in factories and mines. But in 1882, Congress passed the Chinese Exclusion Act, barring immigrants from China. (The ban was repealed in 1943.) Opposition intensified as immigration soared in the early 20th century. In 1907, the peak year for immigration, almost 1.3 million people arrived.

Throughout American history, there has always been a battle over immigration.

In the 1920s, Congress imposed quotas that sharply reduced the number of immigrants and gave preference to northern Europeans over everyone else. The quotas worked against southern and Eastern Europeans. During World War II (1939–45), the quotas prevented millions of Jews and other refugees from escaping the Holocaust. In 1965, the U.S. eliminated quotas, leading to an influx of arrivals from Asia and Latin America.

In recent years, much of the immigration debate has focused on people—largely from Mexico, Central America, and China—who cross the border illegally or stay after their temporary visas expire.

As president, Trump has cracked down on the estimated 11 million undocumented immigrants in the U.S. Americans are divided about whether undocumented immigrants should be forced to leave. Many say they are good for the economy because they fill jobs that Americans don't want, and they often have skills that the U.S. economy needs. Others say people here illegally compete with Americans for jobs and drain the country's resources.

Democrats have generally favored some kind of path toward legalization for those here illegally, provided they learn English. But many Republicans say that would reward those who have broken the law, so the priority should be on tightening border security.

What to Do About the "Dreamers"

There has been more sympathy across party lines for young people brought to the U.S. illegally by their parents as children because they are here through no fault of their own. These so-called Dreamers have been protected since 2012 by a program known as DACA—Deferred Action for Childhood Arrivals—that President Barack Obama (2009–17) created. DACA has shielded them from deportation and allowed them to work in the U.S. legally. President Trump has tried to end the program, and the issue has been tied up in court. He has also claimed that immigration allows criminals into the country and moved to sharply reduce the number of legal immigrants as well.

Others see robust immigration as critical to America's future. They point out that many of America's most innovative companies, such as Google, Apple, Amazon, eBay, Yahoo, and Tesla, were founded by immigrants or their children.

Immigrants "have made an enormous contribution," according to Kraut, the historian. "Their talents have helped make us the preeminent society in the world in terms of higher education and advanced research."

Calls to restrict immigration also reflect anxiety about the country's changing demographics: The Pew Research Center projects that by mid-century, whites will make up less than half of the nation's population.

"The immigration debate is bound up with fears about America becoming a majority-minority country," says Gary Gerstle, a professor of history at Cambridge University in England. But Gerstle thinks Americans will eventually put aside their fears, as they did with previous immigrants.

"These moments of transition in America's perception of itself are very trying times," Gerstle says. "But ultimately the new America wins, and the new America turns out to be something the old Americans can live with." ■

BORDER FENCE: Families speak across the border that separates the United States and Mexico in New Mexico.

Perilous Journey

Ginger fled a violent gang that kidnapped her in Honduras.
She crossed illegally into the United States in search of safety.
That was just the beginning of her struggle.

When the opportunity to escape presented itself, Ginger* knew she had to act fast. It might be the last chance she'd ever have.

A few days earlier, Ginger, then 15, had been kidnapped in broad daylight while she was walking home from school in Tegucigalpa (teh-goo-see-GAHL-puh), the capital of Honduras. On that afternoon in November 2017, a woman approached her asking for help. While Ginger was talking to her, a group of men—likely members of a criminal gang or a drug cartel— grabbed her and dragged her away.

They brought her to an abandoned house, where she was held for days with other

*Ginger asked that we not use her last name to protect herself and her family in Honduras.

young kidnap victims. Ginger was certain she was going to be killed. So when no one was looking, she jumped through a window and ran as fast as she could to a local police station. But she soon realized that the officers were not on her side. In Honduras, police are often corrupt and work with the drug cartels. Ginger returned home to her grandfather, who had been frantic with worry.

DANGER ZONE: Many of today's immigrants are from Central America.

Fleeing Central America

Tens of thousands of people in Central America are coming to the United States to get away from this kind of violence and corruption in their home countries.

Not only did the police brush off her story, Ginger was afraid they would return her to the kidnappers if she said too much. There is no justice in my country, she thought.

A few days later, Ginger's grandfather told her she had to leave Honduras for her own safety. Ginger's mother had fled the Central American country years earlier after surviving a violent attack of her own. She was now living illegally in Michigan. Ginger, her grandfather said, must try to join her.

So in January 2018, just after she turned 16, Ginger said goodbye to the only home she had known. Then she set out on a dangerous 3,000-mile journey to the United States.

It might be hard to imagine a teen making such a trek alone. But about 38,000 children from Central America arrived in the U.S. without a parent or guardian in 2018 alone. They're part of a larger surge of people making the journey to the U.S. from that region.

Lives at Risk at Home

Many of those arriving in the United States say their lives are at risk in their home countries, and some ask to be allowed to stay for that reason. The process for doing so is called seeking **asylum**. But as Ginger learned, getting to the U.S. to ask for asylum can be as dangerous as what migrants like her are trying to escape at home.

Ginger technically wasn't by herself on her journey from Honduras to the U.S. Her

IN HONDURAS, police investigate a shooting. Crime and corruption are rampant there and drug cartels have immense power.

grandfather had hired a human smuggler, known as a coyote, to guide her on the trip. The cost was $1,500 in U.S. currency.

Over the course of a grueling 22 days, Ginger traveled by bus, by car, and on foot. She had just one small bag that held three pairs of pants and three shirts. The only shoes she had were the ones on her feet. Some days, Ginger walked so far in those shoes she would get leg cramps painful enough to make her cry.

At night, she and the coyote often slept outside—even though Ginger didn't have a jacket. She was often hungry and thirsty because she wasn't able to carry food or water.

The coyote treated her well, but Ginger lived in a constant state of fear. At night, she hardly slept. There were a lot of other migrants around—including many men—and she was afraid one of them would attack her at night.

After three weeks of travel, Ginger finally arrived at the Rio Grande, the river that marks the border between Texas and Mexico. She got into a boat with four other people to cross the river.

They made it across safely, stepping illegally onto U.S. soil without passing through a U.S. Border Patrol station. Ginger walked for several hours before immigration authorities spotted her. Exhausted and terrified, she didn't run.

Once in the custody of Border Patrol agents, Ginger was taken to an immigration facility where many other migrants were being held. She slept on the floor that night.

The following day, Ginger was transferred to a large detention facility in Texas where other children who had traveled alone from Central America were being held. While there, Ginger began communicating with her mother. After two months at the detention facility, in April 2018, Ginger was put on a plane to Michigan so she could go live with her mother.

On to Michigan, and College

A week after being reunited with her mother, Ginger enrolled in a local high school. It was lonely at first because she didn't speak English and she couldn't talk to anyone. But after a few days, some students who spoke Spanish befriended her. Along with her new teachers, they started helping her learn English. Things got better after that.

Not long after Ginger arrived in Michigan, her mother's boyfriend heard about a local lawyer who helps undocumented immigrants apply for asylum in the U.S. After hearing Ginger's story, the lawyer agreed to take her case.

With her lawyer's help, Ginger was granted "special immigrant juvenile status," which is for young people who have been abandoned by a parent, in this case her father. She can't be deported back to Honduras unless she commits a crime. In a few years she will be able to get a green card, which is the unofficial name for the permit that lets immigrants permanently live and work in the United States. And eventually she will be able to apply for citizenship.

Ginger knows that some Americans feel hostility toward immigrants like her who have entered the United States illegally. She wants people to know that she came here because of the injustices in her country. Ginger hopes to go to college and become a psychologist and help people heal from traumatic experiences—the way she's healing now.

Despite the uncertainties she faces, Ginger knows in her heart that it was worth risking her life to come to the U.S. Here, she finally feels safe. ■

14TH AMENDMENT: If you're born in the United States, you're a citizen, period.

Should Birthright Citizenship Be Abolished?

Birthright citizenship has been the law since the 14th Amendment* to the U.S. Constitution was adopted in 1868. It says that all people born in the United States are automatically American citizens, regardless of whether their parents are citizens or whether they are authorized to live in the United States. But giving American-born children of undocumented immigrants American citizenship at birth has become a subject of controversy. President Donald Trump has vowed to end birthright citizenship.

** The amendment reads, "All persons born or **naturalized** in the United States and subject to the jurisdiction thereof, are citizens of the United States and of the State wherein they reside."*

Turn the page to see how the two sides present their arguments in this debate. →

DEBATE

 As recently as 2016, over 4 million children born in the United States had at least one undocumented parent. Currently, those babies are automatically U.S. citizens, with all the financial, legal, and social benefits of being an American.

This ability to gain U.S. citizenship has encouraged foreigners to come to the U.S. in order to have babies (often referred to by opponents of birthright citizenship as "anchor babies"). They get citizenship for their children without going through the process of applying for citizenship. President Trump has referred to this loophole as "a magnet for illegal immigration" and is proposing steps to limit it, including screening pregnant women before they're allowed to enter the U.S.

Former senator David Vitter (R-Louisiana) claims birthright citizenship is "a misreading of the 14th Amendment." He and others believe that Congress has the authority to pass laws specifying exactly who is eligible for American citizenship.

> **Congress has the authority to clarify the meaning of the 14th Amendment.**

President Trump has said since his 2016 campaign that he would abolish birthright citizenship in order to discourage illegal immigration. He has suggested he could simply issue an executive order.

The United States long provided a path to citizenship for any immigrant who is willing to legally pursue it. We should reserve citizenship for the children of citizens, and those willing to take on the challenges of becoming a citizen. That would ensure that the privileges of American citizenship and all the benefits that come with it remain protected, and are not given to anyone just because of where they happen to be born. Too many people are exploiting birthright citizenship, and it's changing the fabric of our nation. ■

DEBATE POINTS

★ Birthright citizenship encourages illegal immigration.
★ The 14th Amendment allows Congress to decide the birthright citizenship question.
★ All immigrants should have to apply for citizenship, as should their children, regardless of where they are born.

 **Birthright citizenship is a fundamental part of American society and history and is protected by the Constitution.** As a nation in many ways founded by immigrants, the U.S. depends on the contributions immigrants make to our economy and our culture. The 14th Amendment (1868) granted citizenship to emancipated slaves after the Civil War. It protects all children born in the U.S. by granting them citizenship, regardless of how their parents came to the U.S.

Isaac Naranjo was born in Miami, Florida, in 1999 after his mother came to the U.S. from Ecuador in the 1990s and overstayed her visa. He was five when his family was the subject of an Immigration and Customs Enforcement (ICE) raid targeting his mother (who was allowed to stay).

In college in 2018, Naranjo told the *New York Times*, "I was fortunate enough to have the 14th Amendment to protect me. As a result, I was able to go to high school without fear of ever being deported and am now studying at Berkeley."

The drive to end birthright citizenship is just a tactic in the war against immigration, both legal and illegal. Alex Nowrasteh wrote in the *American Conservative*, "Denying birthright citizenship to the children of noncitizens born here would blunt that exceptional American tradition of assimilation."

This is not a new debate. Several cases questioning birthright citizenship have come before the Supreme Court. The court has consistently ruled that the 14th Amendment protects birthright citizenship.

"As Americans, we must honor the 14th Amendment," says Michele Waslin of George Mason University in Virginia, "and ensure that all people born in the U.S. are citizens, and that no state or individual can again redefine citizenship to create an underclass." ■

The Supreme Court has consistently upheld birthright citizenship.

DEBATE POINTS
★ Birthright citizenship is clearly protected by the 14th Amendment.
★ It protects all children born in the U.S., regardless of how or when their parents got here.
★ Attacking birthright citizenship is just another tactic in the current attempt to limit both legal and illegal immigration.

An Open Door?

The United States prides itself on being a nation of immigrants. But Americans have long been divided about what kind of immigration to allow and from where. In recent years, part of the debate has centered on the soaring number of Central Americans seeking asylum in the U.S.

There are also many people seeking asylum from other parts of the world experiencing violence or war. Many come from Syria, Iraq, and other parts of the Middle East, as well as a number of countries in Africa, that have been devastated by civil wars, ISIS, religious violence, and other conflicts in recent years.

This surge has raised many difficult questions: Who deserves asylum? How can we make applying for asylum fair while preventing abuse of the system?

These two cartoons present different perspectives on immigration. The top cartoon comments on the idea of America as a nation of immigrants. The bottom cartoon features Uncle Sam, a symbol of the United States, and focuses on the situation at the U.S. border with Mexico. ■

Analyze the Cartoons

1. Who are the people in the top cartoon? What is going on there?

2. How does what is being said comment on today's immigration debate?

3. In the bottom cartoon, what has just happened to Uncle Sam?

4. What do you think the cartoonist is saying about the asylum process? Do you agree?

THE INTERNET, especially social media, knows more about you than you may think.

THERE ARE WAYS to limit how much of your personal information is shared online. (See p. 208.)

THINK BEFORE YOU SHARE: When you spread false information, you're contributing to the problem. (See p. 205.)

You and the Media
How to be a smart consumer

FIND MORE ONLINE: www.scholastic.com/howamericaworks

GLOBAL WARMING KILLED OFF SPACE ALIENS

Loch Ness Monster is Real! Huge Skeleton DISCOVERED IN SCOTLAND

HUGE ASTEROID IS HEADED TOWARDS EARTH!

FIDGET SPINNERS GIVE YOU CANCER, RESEARCH REVEALS

READER BEWARE: It's not always obvious what's real and what's fake online.

Telling Fact from Fiction Online

Made-up stories are taking over your news feed. How can you tell what's fact—and protect yourself from fiction?

You're scrolling through your Twitter feed when all of a sudden, you see a shocking headline: "England BANS VIDEO GAMES!!" Outraged, you text your friends, who text their friends. Could the United States be next?

Soon, millions of people are sharing the article online. Within hours, the story has gone viral. There's just one problem. The article is fake, and you, and millions of others around the world, fell for it.

Made-up stories like that one are designed to look real but are completely or partly untrue. Sometimes it's easy to tell when an article is fake—words might be misspelled or randomly capitalized, or the headline might contain multiple exclamation points. But more often than not, fake-news writers are careful to make their stories seem real by including headlines, details, and data that sound believable.

Fake News Can Affect Elections

Such articles may seem harmless, but they can have real consequences. For example, false stories likely influenced the 2016 U.S. presidential election. During the campaign, made-up articles about the two main candidates—Donald Trump and Hillary Clinton—were shared on Facebook nearly 38 million times, with Russia the source of many of them. Similar deceptive stories popped up in the 2020 presidential election.

This is a major problem, says Alan C. Miller. He's the founder of the News Literacy Project, which helps students learn how to spot misinformation. Part of being a good citizen means knowing what's happening in the world—and being mindful that not everything we see on the internet and social media is true.

"The overwhelming majority of information available online has not been verified," says Miller. "It has not been approved by an editor or signed off on by a fact-checker. So we all need to have a healthy amount of skepticism about what we see."

Revolutionary Fake News from Ben Franklin

Influencing people with fake stories has actually been around for centuries. During the American Revolution (1775–83), Benjamin Franklin himself spread false stories. He attempted to increase support for the war by writing articles that falsely claimed that the British had teamed up with Native Americans to murder colonial women and children.

In the late 1800s, newspapers competed for readers by printing shocking headlines and overdramatizing stories. Sometimes reporters made up quotes and cited experts who didn't exist. For example, around the time of the Spanish-American War (1898), several major newspapers published false or exaggerated stories about Spain's mistreatment of its colonists in Cuba. The practice came to be known as yellow journalism.

But fake news really took off with the rise of the internet and social media. When your parents and grandparents were kids, most people got their news from respected newspapers or national news shows on major TV networks.

Beware: "The overwhelming majority of information available online has not been verified."

For the most part, that news came straight from professional journalists who had been trained to conduct thorough research, interview experts, fact-check their stories, and then report the facts while doing their best to keep personal feelings out of their work.

SMART DOG! Fake news isn't always this harmless.

Today, however, almost anyone can write and post articles online. There are thousands of fake news sites, many with official-sounding names. Of course, there are also plenty of trustworthy news sites, including the *New York Times* (nytimes.com), the *Wall Street Journal* (wsj.com), *BBC News* (bbc.com), and *Junior Scholastic* (junior.scholastic.com), just to name a few.

In addition, many politicians have begun using the term "fake news" to refer to factual stories they simply disagree with or don't like. That's making it even harder for Americans to tell fact from fiction—and discouraging people from believing stories that are real.

Why Post Fake Stories: Power and Money

Why do people post fake stories? During election campaigns, it's a way to influence how people vote. That's apparently what the Russians were trying to do in the 2016 and 2020 U.S. elections.

In other cases, the reason for posting fake stories is simple: money. Online advertising is a huge business—and websites that get a lot of visitors can charge more money to run ads. The more visitors a site has, the more views the ads get.

And fake news can attract lots of readers by posting stories with crazy headlines that people are likely to click on and share. "I make like $10,000 a month," fake-news writer Paul Horner told the *Washington Post*.

In fact, one study from the Massachusetts Institute of Technology (MIT) found that on Twitter, false stories spread six times as fast as factual ones—and reach far more readers. MIT researchers discovered that, on average, a false story can spread to 1,500 Twitter users in just 10 hours. By comparison, a factual story can take 60 hours to reach that many people.

The good news is that a lot is being done to stop the spread of fake news. In recent years, for example, Google and Facebook have banned fake news sites from advertising on their sites. Facebook is also working with fact-checking organizations, including PolitiFact. com and FactCheck.org, to help identify and delete made-up articles.

In the end, however, it's up to each of us to be skeptical of what we see online. For starters, if a story doesn't seem quite right or appears too good to be true, investigate it. Spend a few minutes researching the headline, the author, the sources, and the site it came from. And if you suspect a story might be false, don't share it on social media.

"It's our responsibility to stop the spread of fake news," says Jonathan Anzalone of the Center for News Literacy at Stony Brook University in New York. "We need to be committed to seeking out the truth." ∎

HOW TO SPOT A FAKE STORY

Many people can't tell the difference between a factual story and a fake one. But there are easy ways to figure it out. Just ask yourself these questions.

Who's behind the article?

Start by researching the author of the story and the website it came from. Does the writer or site often publish stories making obviously outlandish claims? Also, look at the URL. Sites ending in .com.co often can't be trusted.

What's the evidence?

Evaluate whether the writer has backed up his or her claims with valid reasons and facts. What sources does the author cite—and are they trustworthy? Does the writer quote experts qualified to comment on the topic?

What do other sources say?

Conduct research to find out whether respected news outlets have published the same information, or try to verify the story on a fact-checking website, such as PolitiFact.com or FactCheck.org.

THE REAL PHOTO was taken off the coast of South Africa by a professional photographer in 2005.

REAL

FAKE

THIS PHONY SHARK photo often goes viral after big storms. The location has been identified as New Jersey, Puerto Rico, and Texas.

When Photos Lie

Fake images are tricking countless people on social media. Here's why that matters—and how you can avoid getting fooled.

The incredible image appeared on Twitter hours after Hurricane Harvey struck Texas in August 2017. In the photo (above), a great white shark swims alongside drivers on a flooded Houston highway. It's no surprise that hundreds of thousands of people clicked on the post, and many shared it. The picture was even broadcast on national news.

The problem? The image was fake. A hoaxster had used photo-editing software to insert the shark into a picture of a flooded road.

The shark shot is one example of a fast-growing problem in the digital age: phony photos. As tech tools once available only to pros become more accessible, just about anyone can alter photographs.

Some doctored images are meant to be a joke (a shot of your birthday party with

Beyoncé or Stephen Curry added in). But others are created to spread lies and stir up controversy. Russian operatives, for instance, filled social media with phony images as part of an effort to influence the 2016 U.S. presidential election.

Like other kinds of fake news, manipulated photos can make people believe things that aren't true. They can be even more powerful than fake articles because many people are more likely to trust a photo. Plus, images instantly arouse strong feelings in people, says John Silva of the nonprofit News Literacy Project. "With the right image and the right headline," he says, "you can manipulate people's emotions and make them believe all sorts of things."

Why Fakes Seem Real

It's not always easy to spot a fake. In a study by Warwick University in England, people could identify manipulated images only about 60 percent of the time. Even when people did detect a phony pic, most couldn't pinpoint what had been altered.

Many sham photos seem authentic because they were created from real images that have been changed only slightly. For example, in March 2018, a fake picture surfaced on Twitter of teen gun-control activist Emma González appearing to tear up a copy of the U.S. Constitution (below, left). The real photo shows González, a survivor of the Parkland, Florida, school shooting a month earlier, ripping a gun-range target.

IN THIS ALTERED photo of activist Emma González, a ripped gun-range target was replaced with the Constitution. Her face was widened and shadows were added under her eyes.

FAKE

REAL

THE REAL PHOTO was published by *Teen Vogue*.

HOW TO TAKE CONTROL OF YOUR DATA

Here are some steps you can take to limit the data you share.

• DENY ACCESS

When you install an app on your phone, you're often asked to give that app access to, say, your photos or address book. Some access is necessary for an app to function. For example, Snapchat wouldn't be useful without access to your camera. But some apps ask for permissions they don't really need.

• OPT OUT

You can see which apps have access to your Facebook data by going to the Apps option in your Settings. You can cut off apps from grabbing your data by tapping the X button next to the app. You can also control which apps have access to your Google account by going to the "Apps with access to your account" page.

• CRUNCH COOKIES

Third-party cookies allow companies to dig up data on internet users. Most internet browsers allow you to delete or limit cookies. Search under Tools or Settings for a Privacy category. Blocking all cookies may make it difficult to use some websites, so look for a setting that blocks third-party cookies.

MANY APPS ASK before accessing your data, and you don't have to say yes.

The fake was posted by a bot (or robot) account on Twitter. It prompted outrage, and that's the goal of many fake photos: to stir up strong feelings around hot-button issues. In this case, the phony image reinforced fears some Americans have about losing their Second Amendment rights. That made them less skeptical of the altered photo.

"When an image hits a belief that we already have, we will readily accept it," Silva says. "And we will share it."

Fake Photos and Elections

Could a bogus photo influence who you vote for? Russian operatives hoped so during the 2016 U.S. presidential campaign. They used false images in an attempt to sway Americans to vote for Donald Trump.

For example, as Trump promised to crack down on illegal immigration, a Russia-backed Facebook account posted a photo that appeared to show a woman and child at a pro-immigration rally with a sign reading, "Give me more free [stuff]." The hackers had digitally altered an old image. In reality, what the woman's sign said was, "No human being is illegal."

Fake photos worry experts for many reasons. For one thing, people are more likely to share images than text on social media, so phony pics spread quickly. Plus, exposure to all those frauds can make us doubt real news photos.

In addition, tech companies—still struggling with how to combat fake news articles—are even less equipped to deal with fake images. Facebook has expanded its fact-checking program to include photos and videos. But those efforts still depend largely on people doing the verifying—and that takes time.

The best defense against fake photos may be taking a minute to consider images you see on social media before reposting them, especially ones that seem shocking or are getting a lot of attention.

"If you're having a very strong reaction, that's a warning sign," says Silva. "You need to sit back from your screen and start asking questions." ∎

PHOTO TIP
- **DRAG AND DROP** any image into the search box on **images.google.com** to help determine if a photo is a fake.

"When an image hits a belief that we already have, we will readily accept it."

WHAT SOCIAL MEDIA KNOWS ABOUT ME

Gregory Gottfried downloaded all the information that Facebook had on him. The results were frightening.

If you want to find out what Facebook knows about you, the company has now made it easy, providing a tool on its site. But be forewarned: It might creep you out, as it did to me when I downloaded my data in 2018.

Starting when I created my account on July 28, 2009, Facebook has been keeping track of every one of my likes, posts, photos, and searches. It knows what ads have appeared on my page and whether I've clicked on them. It knows all the contacts on my phone—names and numbers. It knows I'm a runner (because of my connected app Runkeeper), some of my TV habits (I liked Conan O'Brien's page), and some of my favorite restaurants and stores. (I've clicked on an ad for Chick-fil-A and searched for Nike.)

It knows more intimate details too. If I searched for someone—perhaps a crush—Facebook has kept count, and it knows whether she ever searched for me. Luckily, I never connected my Location Services to the app, so Facebook doesn't know my location every second of every day. But it does know every city I've logged in from.

With Facebook, I know that every move I make has the possibility of being tracked. But seeing everything laid out in front of me was jarring. All my information—including the unique numerical code Facebook assigned to me, which enables it to recognize my face in photos—was right there. It feels as though I gave up a chunk of my identity to view videos of puppies and argue about politics.

To see what Facebook has on you, go to the desktop version of the site and click Settings in the drop-down menu on the right side of the screen. Underneath General Account Settings, choose the link to "Download a copy of your Facebook data." From there, click Create File, and after a bit of downloading, you can cringe at posts Facebook has archived from your first day on the site. Good luck—and brace yourself! ∎

Gregory Gottfried was an intern at The New York Times Upfront. *He graduated from the Columbia Journalism School in New York and is now a web producer and writer at* Golf Digest.

Is Social Media Good for Democracy?

Social media platforms like Snapchat, Instagram, and Twitter have revolutionized how we communicate. Facebook has an estimated 2.3 billion users worldwide, Instagram has 1 billion, and Twitter has 326 million. These platforms have allowed millions of people around the world to debate issues facing the U.S. and the world.

But these same platforms have allowed foreign countries to manipulate American presidential elections. They can also serve as global megaphones for extremists, hate groups, and terrorists. And we're still trying to figure out whose responsibility it is to police social media: Users? The platforms themselves? The government?

With all these issues in mind, do you think social media strengthens or weakens democracy?

Turn the page to see how the two sides present their arguments in this debate. ➜

YES **The internet and now social media have given the public incredible access to information about the activities of their governments and candidates running for office in a way that was never before possible.**

What's more, we get to speak out about them and share our opinions with friends and strangers alike. If we care to, we can try to convince others of our views about those issues that are important to us all.

Social media holds news outlets and politicians alike to higher levels of scrutiny and accountability. Before the internet and social media, people were largely limited to local media, and "conversations" with politicians were largely one way.

Now, it's not only much easier to find information about any government official's views and record, it's also easier to find media from across the country—or across the globe—to help understand and analyze that information. Of course, social media also offers the ability to engage with other people—who may or may not have the same views.

These platforms also give people more access to the government itself and to candidates. This direct line gives the public the ability to actually talk to government officials and voters the ability to engage with candidates for office: It's no longer a one-way conversation, and that makes the discussions much more powerful.

Social media has also played a critical role in spreading the word and gaining support for social and political movements from March for Our Lives and Black Lives Matter, to #MeToo and the Tea Party.

What may be most significant about this vastly expanded access is that it's essentially available to everyone, regardless of age, ethnicity, education, or economic status. That makes social media the most democratic of institutions. ◼

> ## Social media has made people more connected to their governments.

DEBATE POINTS
- ★ **News outlets and government officials can be held to greater account for their actions and statements.**
- ★ **Conversations between candidates and constituents are no longer one-way.**
- ★ **Social media has helped social and political movements, both left and right, gain traction.**

NO

Democracy depends on free and fair elections. The U.S. presidential election in 2016 fell prey to lies and **propaganda** spread by foreign powers through social media.

Social media is a powerful tool for spreading information, but it's an equally powerful tool for spreading misinformation, and in the process, hurting democracy.

A country like Russia now has not only the desire but also the means to subvert the truth. In 2016 Russian operatives were able to create fake accounts on Facebook, Twitter, and Instagram to spread false information about the candidates and issues in the U.S. presidential election.

This misinformation fueled conspiracy theories, deepened our social and political divisions, and discouraged people from voting. Other countries and extremist groups have noted the impact of Russia's misinformation campaign, and are now following in its footsteps.

In some ways, social media platforms are in a no-win situation. They get criticized for taking no action against false or extreme views, but if they take a more active role policing their platforms, they can be accused of censorship.

Others accuse social media companies of turning a blind eye to these issues to focus on their profits.

"Because social media platforms depend on advertising to make money, they're designed to manipulate users' attention," says Roger McNamee, the author of *Zucked: Waking Up to the Facebook Catastrophe.*

In other words, opinions that make you really happy or really angry (the ones that are also more likely to be exaggerated or false) get the most attention, and generate the most page views—of the content and the ads.

TV and print ads also want to generate attention, but they are covered by rules regarding the truth, so why not online ads as well? At the very least, social media needs more oversight and regulations to provide a more honest product to its users. ■

Social media doesn't encourage the civil debate that democracy requires.

DEBATE POINTS

★ Social media is filled with misinformation directly targeting the public.
★ Foreign powers have already tampered with U.S. elections via social media.
★ The reliance of social media companies on advertising results in greater polarization on the issues of the day.

No Secrets

If you're reading this sentence, that's a good thing: It probably means you put down your phone for a minute. (And yes, it means the writer put down his phone for a minute!) We've all grown attached to the internet in its many forms, and the internet has grown attached to us—for better or worse, as you've read in this unit. It's also given cartoonists plenty to comment on.

Internet and marketing companies have access to all sorts of information about us, as individuals and groups, with varying degrees of privacy protection in place. But how do they get all that information? These two cartoonists have some fun with that question, although the implications of their message may not be so funny. ■

Analyze the Cartoons

1. What's happening to the people in the top cartoon? How are they reacting?

2. In the bottom cartoon it seems there are two searches going on. What are they?

3. What are some of the pros and cons of all the information we provide to internet and marketing companies through our use of the internet?

WELCOME ABOARD! Two very happy new Americans show off their citizenship papers at a naturalization ceremony in Miami Beach, Florida.

SINCE THE FIRST naturalization law in 1790, all new citizens have taken an oath to support the Constitution.

Could You Pass America's Citizenship Test?

If you're in an American classroom, odds are you were born here and didn't have to "test in" to be become a citizen. Immigrants have it a lot tougher.

NEW CITIZENS after taking the Oath of Allegiance at Mount Vernon, George Washington's home in Virginia, on July 4, 2018

How to Become a U.S. Citizen

Becoming a U.S. citizen isn't easy. Before they can even take the citizenship test, immigrants must overcome many hurdles.

f you were born in the United States, American citizenship is probably something you take for granted. You have what's called birthright citizenship, meaning your citizenship is automatic.

It's different for immigrants. About 700,000 people a year complete the long process of becoming naturalized citizens. Applicants must have immigrated legally and been permanent residents for five years; they must not have committed any serious crimes; and they undergo identity and security checks. They must prove they can read, write, and speak basic English, and they must pass a civics test: They are asked 10 questions, in an oral exam, from a list of 100 and must answer at least six correctly. (The questions and answers are available online.)

How well would you do if you had to pass the test to become a citizen?

Topics on the U.S. Citizenship Test

All topics, questions, and answers on pages 219–230 are taken directly from the website of the U.S. Citizenship and Immigration Services (my.uscis.gov/prep/test/civics).

AMERICAN GOVERNMENT

A. Principles of American Democracy

B. System of Government

C. Rights and Responsibilities

AMERICAN HISTORY

A. Colonial Period and Independence

B. The 1800s

C. Recent American History and Other Important Historical Information

CIVICS

A. Geography

B. Symbols

C. Holidays

The Test

How many of the 100 questions can you answer correctly?

AMERICAN GOVERNMENT

A: Principles of American Democracy

1. What is the supreme law of the land?

2. What does the Constitution do?

3. The idea of self-government is in the first three words of the Constitution. What are these words?

4. What is an amendment?

5. What do we call the first 10 amendments to the Constitution?

6. What is one right or freedom from the First Amendment?*

7. How many amendments does the Constitution have?

8. What did the Declaration of Independence do?

9. What are two rights in the Declaration of Independence?

10. What is freedom of religion?

11. What is the economic system in the United States?*

12. What is the "rule of law"?

*If you are 65 years old or older and have been a legal permanent resident of the U.S. for 20 or more years, you may study just the questions that have been marked with an asterisk.

B: System of Government

13. Name one branch or part of the government.

14. What stops one branch of government from becoming too powerful?

15. Who is in charge of the executive branch?

16. Who makes federal laws?

17. What are the two parts of the U.S. Congress?*

18. How many U.S. senators are there?

19. We elect a U.S. senator for how many years?

20. Who is one of your state's U.S. senators now?*

21. The House of Representatives has how many voting members?

22. We elect a U.S. representative for how many years?

23. Name your U.S. representative.

24. Who does a U.S. senator represent?

25. Why do some states have more representatives than other states?

26. We elect a president for how many years?

27. In what month do we vote for president?*

28. What is the name of the president of the United States now?*

29. What is the name of the vice president of the United States now?

30. If the president can no longer serve, who becomes president?

31. If both the president and the vice president can no longer serve, who becomes president?

32. Who is the commander in chief of the military?

33. Who signs bills to become laws?

34. Who vetoes bills?

35. What does the president's cabinet do?

36. What are two cabinet-level positions?

37. What does the judicial branch do?

38. What is the highest court in the United States?

39. How many justices are on the Supreme Court?

40. Who is the chief justice of the United States now?

41. Under our Constitution, some powers belong to the federal government. What is one power of the federal government?

42. Under our Constitution, some powers belong to the states. What is one power of the states?

43. Who is the governor of your state now?

44. What is the capital of your state?*

45. What are the two major political parties in the United States?*

46. What is the political party of the president now?

47. What is the name of the Speaker of the House of Representatives now?

C: Rights and Responsibilities

48. There are four amendments to the Constitution about who can vote. Describe one of them.

49. What is one responsibility that is only for United States citizens?*

50. Name one right only for United States citizens.

51. What are two rights of everyone living in the United States?

52. What do we show loyalty to when we say the Pledge of Allegiance?

53. What is one promise you make when you become a United States citizen?

54. How old do citizens have to be to vote for president?*

55. What are two ways that Americans can participate in their democracy?

56. When is the last day you can send in federal income tax forms?*

57. When must all men register for the Selective Service?

AMERICAN HISTORY

A: Colonial Period and Independence

58. What is one reason colonists came to America?

59. Who lived in America before the Europeans arrived?

60. What group of people was taken to America and sold as slaves?

61. Why did the colonists fight the British?

62. Who wrote the Declaration of Independence?

63. When was the Declaration of Independence adopted?

64. There were 13 original states. Name three.

65. What happened at the Constitutional Convention?

66. When was the Constitution written?

67. The Federalist Papers supported the passage of the U.S. Constitution. Name one of the writers.

68. What is one thing Benjamin Franklin is famous for?

69. Who is the Father of Our Country?

70. Who was the first president?

B: 1800s

71. What territory did the United States buy from France in 1803?

72. Name one war fought by the United States in the 1800s.

73. Name the U.S. war between the North and the South.

74. Name one problem that led to the Civil War.

75. What was one important thing that Abraham Lincoln did?*

76. What did the Emancipation Proclamation do?

77. What did Susan B. Anthony do?

C: Recent American History and Other Important Historical Information

78. Name one war fought by the United States in the 1900s.*

79. Who was president during World War I?

80. Who was president during the Great Depression and World War II?

89. What ocean is on the west coast of the United States?

90. What ocean is on the east coast of the United States?

91. Name one U.S. territory.

92. Name one state that borders Canada.

93. Name one state that borders Mexico.

94. What is the capital of the United States?*

95. Where is the Statue of Liberty?*

81. Who did the United States fight in World War II?

82. Before he was president, Dwight D. Eisenhower was a general. What war was he in?

83. During the Cold War, what was the main concern of the United States?

84. What movement tried to end racial discrimination?

85. What did Martin Luther King Jr. do?*

86. What major event happened on September 11, 2001, in the United States?

87. Name one Native American group in the United States.

CIVICS

A: Geography

88. Name one of the two longest rivers in the United States.

B: Symbols

96. Why does the flag have 13 stripes?

97. Why does the flag have 50 stars?*

98. What is the name of the national anthem?

C: Holidays

99. When do we celebrate Independence Day?*

100. Name two national U.S. holidays.

The Answers (Don't Peek!)

AMERICAN GOVERNMENT

A: Principles of American Democracy

1. the Constitution
2. sets up the government; defines the government; protects basic rights of Americans
3. We the People
4. a change (to the Constitution); an addition (to the Constitution)
5. the Bill of Rights
6. speech, religion, assembly, press, petition the government
7. 27
8. announced our independence (from Great Britain); declared our independence (from Great Britain); said that the United States is free (from Great Britain)
9. life, liberty, pursuit of happiness
10. You can practice any religion, or not practice a religion.
11. capitalist economy, market economy
12. Everyone must follow the law; leaders must obey the law; government must obey the law; no one is above the law.

B: System of Government

13. Congress, legislative; president, executive; the courts, judicial
14. checks and balances, separation of powers
15. the president
16. Congress; Senate and House (of Representatives); (U.S. or national) legislature
17. the Senate and House (of Representatives)

*Some answers change with time depending on who is currently in office at the time the test is given.

18. one hundred (100)

19. 6

20. Answers will vary; District of Columbia residents and residents of U.S. territories should answer that D.C., or the territory where the applicant lives, has no U.S. senators.

21. 435

22. 2

23. Answers will vary; residents of territories with nonvoting delegates or resident commissioners may provide the name of that delegate or commissioner. Also acceptable is any statement that the territory has no (voting) representatives in Congress.

24. all people of the state

25. (because of) the state's population; (because) they have more people; (because) some states have more people

26. 4

27. November

28. Donald Trump*

29. Mike Pence*

30. the vice president

31. the Speaker of the House

32. the president

33. the president

34. the president

35. advises the president

36. secretary of agriculture, secretary of commerce, secretary of defense, secretary of education, secretary of energy, secretary of health and human services, secretary of homeland security, secretary of housing and urban development, secretary of the interior, secretary of labor, secretary of state, secretary of transportation, secretary of the treasury, secretary of veterans affairs, attorney general, vice president

37. reviews laws, explains laws, resolves disputes (disagreements), decides if a law goes against the Constitution

38. the Supreme Court

39. Visit uscis.gov/citizenship/testupdates for the number of justices on the Supreme Court.

40. John Roberts*

C: Rights and Responsibilities

48. Citizens 18 and older (can vote); you don't have to pay (a poll tax) to vote; any citizen can vote (women and men can vote); a male citizen of any race (can vote).

49. serve on a jury, vote in a federal election

50. vote in a federal election, run for federal office

51. freedom of expression, freedom of speech, freedom of assembly, freedom to petition the government, freedom of religion, the right to bear arms

52. the United States, the flag

53. give up loyalty to other countries; defend the Constitution and laws of the United States; obey the laws of the United States; serve in the

41. to print money; to declare war; to create an army; to make treaties

42. provide schooling and education; provide protection (police); provide safety (fire departments); grant driver's licenses, approve zoning and land use

43. Answers will vary; District of Columbia residents should answer that D.C. does not have a governor.

44. Answers will vary; District of Columbia residents should answer that D.C. is not a state and does not have a capital; residents of U.S. territories should name the capital of the territory.

45. Democratic and Republican

46. Republican

47. Nancy Pelosi*

U.S. military (if needed); serve (do important work for) the nation (if needed); be loyal to the United States

54. 18 and older

55. vote; join a political party; help with a campaign; join a civic group; join a community group; give an elected official your opinion on an issue; call senators and representatives; publicly support or oppose an issue or policy; run for office; write to a newspaper

56. April 15

57. at age 18, between 18 and 26

AMERICAN HISTORY

A: Colonial Period and Independence

58. freedom, political liberty, religious freedom, economic opportunity, practice their religion, escape persecution

59. American Indians, Native Americans

60. Africans, people from Africa

61. because of high taxes (taxation without representation); because the British army stayed in their houses (boarding, quartering); because they didn't have self-government

62. (Thomas) Jefferson

63. July 4, 1776

64. New Hampshire, Massachusetts, Rhode Island, Connecticut, New York, New Jersey, Pennsylvania, Delaware, Maryland, Virginia, North Carolina, South Carolina, Georgia

65. The Constitution was written; the Founding Fathers wrote the Constitution.

66. 1787

67. (James) Madison, (Alexander) Hamilton, (John) Jay, Publius

68. U.S. diplomat; oldest member of

Revolutionary War Battles

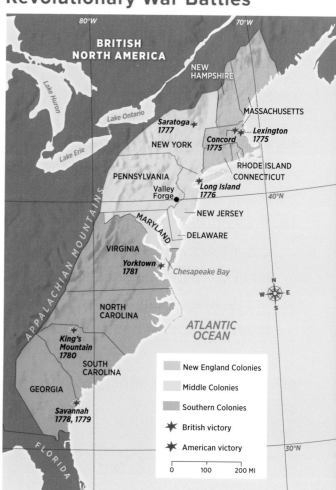

the Constitutional Convention; first postmaster general of the United States; writer of *Poor Richard's Almanac*; started the first free libraries

69. (George) Washington

70. (George) Washington

B: 1800s

71. the Louisiana Territory, Louisiana

72. War of 1812, Mexican-American War, Civil War, Spanish-American War

73. the Civil War, the War between the States

74. slavery, economic reasons, states' rights

75. freed the slaves (Emancipation Proclamation); saved (or preserved) the Union; led the United States during the Civil War

76. freed the slaves; freed slaves in the Confederacy; freed slaves in the Confederate states; freed slaves in most Southern states

77. fought for women's rights, fought for civil rights

C: Recent American History and Other Important Historical Information

78. World War I, World War II, Korean War, Vietnam War, (Persian) Gulf War

79. (Woodrow) Wilson

80. (Franklin) Roosevelt

81. Japan, Germany, and Italy

82. World War II

83. communism

84. civil rights (movement)

85. fought for civil rights, worked for equality for all Americans

86. Terrorists attacked the United States.

87. Cherokee, Navajo, Sioux, Chippewa, Choctaw, Pueblo, Apache, Iroquois, Creek, Blackfeet, Seminole, Cheyenne, Arawak, Shawnee, Mohegan, Huron, Oneida, Lakota, Crow, Teton, Hopi, Inuit

CIVICS

A: Geography

88. Missouri (River), Mississippi (River)

89. Pacific (Ocean)

90. Atlantic (Ocean)

91. Puerto Rico, U.S. Virgin Islands, American Samoa, Northern Mariana Islands, Guam

92. Maine, New Hampshire, Vermont, New York, Pennsylvania, Ohio, Michigan, Minnesota, North Dakota, Montana, Idaho, Washington, Alaska

93. California, Arizona, New Mexico, Texas

94. Washington, D.C.

95. New York (Harbor), Liberty Island; also acceptable are New Jersey, near New York City, and on the Hudson River

B: Symbols

96. because there were 13 original colonies, because the stripes represent the original colonies

97. because each star represents a state, because there are 50 states

98. "The Star-Spangled Banner"

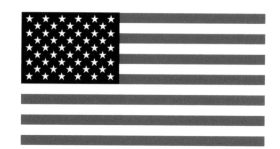

C: Holidays

99. July 4

100. Martin Luther King Jr. Day, Presidents' Day, Memorial Day, Independence Day, Labor Day, Columbus Day, Veterans Day, Thanksgiving, Christmas

We hope that *How America Works* not only helped you do well on this pop quiz, but also gave you a better understanding of our democracy: its many achievements, the work that remains to be done, and how you can advance America's story in the 21st century.

Glossary

acquitted (uh-KWIT-id) found not guilty of a crime

activists (AK-tuh-vists) people who work to bring political or social change

advocates (AD-vuh-kits) people who support an idea or a plan

amendment (uh-MEND-muhnt) a change that is made to a law or a legal document

anonymous (uh-NAH-nuh-muhs) written, done, or given by a person whose name is not known or made public

aristocrat (uh-RIS-tuh-krat) a member of a group of people thought to be the best in some way, usually based on their social class

asylum (uh-SYE-lum) protection given to someone who has left a dangerous place

biased (BYE-uhst) favoring one person or point of view more than another

bipartisan (bye-PAR-tuh-suhn) supported by both major U.S. political parties: the Democrats and the Republicans

censoring (SEN-sur-ing) removing parts of a book, movie, or other work that are thought to be unacceptable or offensive

clause (KLAWZ) a section of a formal legal document

conservative (kuhn-SUR-vuh-tiv) in political views; generally favoring business and smaller government, and being opposed to large government social welfare programs

delegates (DEL-i-guts) people who represent other people at a meeting or in a legislature

doctrine (DAHK-trin) a belief or teaching of a religion, political party, or other group

grassroots (gras-ROOTS) supported and directed by ordinary people

impartial (im-PAHR-shuhl) treating all persons or points of view equally

inaugurated (in-AW-gyuh-ray-tid) sworn into public office with a formal ceremony

incrimination (in-krim-uh-NAY-shuhn) evidence that someone is guilty of something

inherently (in-HARE-uhnt-lee) naturally and characteristically

internment (in-TURN-muhnt) being held as a prisoner

legislatures (LEJ-is-lay-churz) groups of people, usually elected, who have the power to make or change laws for a country or state

minorities (mye-NOR-i-teez) groups of people of a particular race, ethnic group, or religion living among a larger group of a different race, ethnic group, or religion

monolithically (mah-nuh-LITH-ik-lee) as one large group

naturalized (NACH-ur-uh-lyzed) made someone a citizen of a country where they were not born

parliament (PAHR-luh-muhnt) the group of people who have been elected to make the laws in some countries, such as Canada, the United Kingdom, and Israel

picketed (PIK-it-id) stood outside a place in protest

propaganda (prah-puh-GAN-duh) information that is spread to influence the way people think

provision (pruh-VIZH-uhn) something that is named as a condition in an agreement, a law, or a document

quotas (KWOH-tuhz) a specific number or share of something

reservation (rez-ur-VAY-shuhn) an area of land set aside by the government for a special purpose, such as use by Native Americans

segregated (SEG-ri-gay-tid) separated or kept apart from the main group

seizures (SEE-zhurz) situations where government or law enforcement officials take private property from people

suffrage (SUHF-rij) the right to vote

tenure (TEN-yur) the holding of an office or other position

testimony (TES-tuh-moh-nee) a formal statement given by a witness or an expert in a court of law

treaty (TREE-tee) a formal written agreement between two or more countries

unanimous (yoo-NAN-uh-muhs) agreed on by everyone

Learn More

BOOKS

Benoit, Peter. *The Supreme Court.* New York: Scholastic, 2014.

Burgan, Michael. *The Branches of U.S. Government.* New York: Scholastic, 2012.

Burgan, Michael. *The U.S. Constitution.* New York: Scholastic, 2012.

McDaniel, Melissa. *The Declaration of Independence.* New York: Scholastic, 2012.

Zeiger, Jennifer. *The Civil Rights Movement.* New York: Scholastic, 2012.

MAGAZINES

Junior Scholastic, the news and Social Studies resource for grades 6–8, https://junior.scholastic.com/

Scholastic Scope, the multigenre language arts teaching package for grades 6–8, https://scope.scholastic.com/

The New York Times Upfront, the current events magazine for grades 9–12, https://upfront.scholastic.com/

Scholastic Action, the skill-building language arts magazine for striving readers in grades 6–12, https://action.scholastic.com/

Choices, Scholastic's health, social-emotional learning, and life-skills magazine for grades 7–12, https://choices.scholastic.com/

Scholastic Art, bringing classic and contemporary art to life for grades 7–12, https://art.scholastic.com/

Science World, the skill-building science news and nonfiction magazine for grades 6–10, https://scienceworld.scholastic.com/

ONLINE RESOURCES

Visit *www.scholastic.com/howamericaworks* to check out videos, teacher tools, and more.

Index

Numbers in *italic* refer to images.

Magazine and Book Credits

Unit 1: The Declaration of Independence
"Free and Independent States," adapted from "The Declaration of Independence," by Melissa McDaniel (Cornerstones of Freedom series, Scholastic, 2012)
"The American Revolution: 7 Things You Should Know (But Probably Don't)," adapted from Junior Scholastic, Sept. 3, 2018

Unit 2: The Constitution
"How 'We the People' Created the Constitution," adapted from "The U.S. Constitution," by Michael Burgan (Cornerstones of Freedom series, Scholastic, 2012)
"Your 5-Minute Guide to the Constitution," adapted from Junior Scholastic, Sept. 4, 2017
"The ERA Tries for a Comeback," adapted from Junior Scholastic, Sept. 3, 2018

Unit 3: The Bill of Rights
"Your 5-Minute Guide to the Bill of Rights," adapted from Junior Scholastic, Oct. 9, 2017
"First Amendment 101," adapted from Junior Scholastic, Jan. 8, 2018
"Protest Nation!," adapted from Junior Scholastic, May 15, 2017
"The Art of Protest," adapted from Junior Scholastic, May 15, 2017

Unit 4: How Washington Works
"Checks & Balances," adapted from Junior Scholastic, Sept. 4, 2017
"A Day in the Life of a Member of Congress," adapted from Junior Scholastic, Sept. 2, 2019
"A Changing Congress," adapted from Junior Scholastic, Jan. 7, 2019
"I Helped This Teacher Get Elected to Congress," adapted from Junior Scholastic, Jan. 7, 2019

Unit 5: Supreme Court Cases Every Student Should Know
"Your 5-Minute Guide to the Supreme Court," adapted from Junior Scholastic, March 21, 2016
"A Day in the Life of a Supreme Court Justice," adapted from Junior Scholastic, Oct. 14, 2019
"Five Supreme Court Cases That Directly Affect You," adapted from The New York Times Upfront, multiple issues
"Three Cases That Changed America," adapted from Junior Scholastic, March 21, 2016
"1965: A 13-Year-Old Fights for Free Speech," adapted from The New York Times Upfront, Jan. 7, 2019
"1967: The Right to Love," adapted from The New York Times Upfront, Jan. 9, 2017

Unit 6: The Presidency
"Is the Presidency An Impossible Job?" adapted from Junior Scholastic, Feb. 18, 2019
"Electoral College 101," adapted from The New York Times Upfront, Sept. 19, 2016
"How Impeachment Works," adapted from The New York Times Upfront, Oct. 28, 2019
"The Four Presidents Who've Faced Impeachment," adapted from The New York Times Upfront, Oct. 28, 2019

Unit 7: Why Voting Matters
"It's True: Every Vote Counts," adapted from Junior Scholastic, Feb. 19, 2018
"1971: 18-Year-Olds Get the Vote," adapted from The New York Times Upfront, Sept. 5, 2011
"Has a Youth Wave Begun?" adapted from The New York Times Upfront, Jan. 7, 2019
"Teens Head to the Statehouse," adapted from The New York Times Upfront, May 13, 2019

Unit 8: The Long Struggle for Civil Rights
"The Civil Rights Hero You've Never Heard Of," adapted from Junior Scholastic, Feb. 19, 2018
"Luther Standing Bear's Powerful Voice," adapted from Junior Scholastic, Nov. 11, 2019
"The Quest for Women's Equality," adapted from Junior Scholastic, Oct. 10, 2016
"A Bold Act of Solidarity," adapted from The New York Times Upfront, Dec. 9, 2019
"Justice for Farmworkers," adapted from "Cesar Chavez," by Josh Gregory (A True Book, Scholastic, 2015)
"Sitting Down to Take a Stand," adapted from The New York Times Upfront, Jan. 6, 2020
"1960: Ruby Bridges," by Josh Gregory
"1963: The Birmingham Children's Crusade," adapted from Junior Scholastic, Jan. 6, 2020
"A Half-Century after MLK: Where Are We Now?" adapted from The New York Times Upfront, Jan. 29, 2018
"Timeline: Highlights of the Civil Rights Movement," adapted from The New York Times Upfront, Jan. 29, 2018
"Remembering Matthew Shepard," adapted from The New York Times Upfront, Jan. 28, 2019
"Matthew Shepard Was My Friend," adapted from The New York Times Upfront, Jan. 28, 2019

Unit 9: Immigration: Who Gets to Be an American?
"Timeline: Immigration in the U.S.," adapted from The New York Times Upfront, Feb. 19, 2018
"What Makes Immigration So Controversial?" adapted from The New York Times Upfront, Feb. 19, 2018
"Perilous Journey," adapted from The New York Times Upfront, Jan. 7, 2019

Unit 10: You and the Media
"Telling Fact From Fiction Online," adapted from Junior Scholastic, Sept. 23, 2019
"How to Spot a Fake Story," adapted from Junior Scholastic, Sept. 23, 2019
"When Photos Lie," adapted from The New York Times Upfront, Dec. 10, 2018
"How to Take Control of Your Data," adapted from The New York Times Upfront, Sept. 3, 2018
"What Social Media Knows About Me," adapted from The New York Times Upfront, Sept. 3, 2018

Photo Credits